PRIVATE
DREAMS
OF PUBLIC PEOPLE

For my father Jack,

and for The Society for Memorial Sloan-Kettering
for Cancer Research

Text © 2002 Lauren Lawrence
Foreword © 2002 Larry King

© 2002 Assouline Publishing, Inc.
601 West 26th Street
18th floor
New York, NY 10001
USA
Tel.: 212 989-6810   Fax: 212 647-0005
www.assouline.com

ISBN: 2 84323 339 9

Color separation: Gravor (Switzerland)
Printed by Pizzi (Italy)
Proofreading: Jennifer Ditsler

Lauren Lawrence

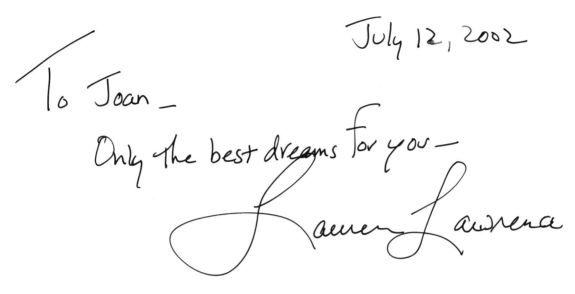

July 12, 2002

To Joan —
Only the best dreams for you —

Lauren Lawrence

PRIVATE
DREAMS
OF PUBLIC PEOPLE

Foreword by Larry King

ASSOULINE

CONTENTS

FOREWORD

I guess everybody dreams. What you are about to read shows how revealing— and in some cases startling—they can be. I can't be in this book because all my life I have had trouble remembering my dreams. It bothers me because I know the subconscious is working and can only be of help. But for the life of me, I can count the dreams I can remember on the fingers of one hand.

I vaguely remember a nightmare I had as a child after seeing the movie *King Kong*. In the dream, the gorilla was in my bedroom. Maybe that kept me from remembering future dreams?

I remember another dream at a time in my life when I was out of work and broke. I dreamt that I found an envelope on the street containing $10,000. I scooped up the money, went home, put it in the breast pocket of a sports jacket and laid in bed pinching myself with joy. As soon as I woke up, I ran to the closet. No envelope. No money. I tore apart the closet (this was a very vivid dream)— nothing. So, as in this case, maybe not remembering is a pretty good idea.

I have done many interviews over the years on the subject and can safely say I've never met anyone who wasn't interested in learning about his or her dreams or the dreams of others, particularly the dreams of celebrities. You will enjoy what you are about to read, and by the way, like the old song says: "I'll see you in my dreams"… maybe.

Larry King

INTRODUCTION

When Sigmund Freud sexualized dreams, the end of the nineteenth century did more than turn, it looked back on itself introspectively. And in an instant the world sat up—pen in hand—and made note of its seductively cloaked evening visitors. When we were told that dreams were unconscious manifestations of our drives and wishful fantasies, dreams became the hot commodity of the moment. Bedrooms filled with unconscious reportage, and symbolism was everywhere. A pipe was no longer just a pipe. Freud told us the dreams of Dora, Little Hans, and the waking dreams of Anna O. But who was Anna O. when she was around? I admit I was somewhat intrigued by her symptoms, but in hindsight, how much more titillating would it have been if Freud had written about the dreams of Dietrich and Von Sternberg, Wallace Simpson and her pale Prince of Wales, the little King who simply would not be.

Celebrities are like dreams in that there is intense interest in their dissection. Yet fame, like gossamer, is not easily anatomized. Magazines and media attempt to demystify the private lives and glamorous facades of movie stars and high-profile individuals, but nudity is never enough, they want to peel back the glossy veneer and gaze underneath the skin as well.

The paparazzi phallic lens zooms into the darkest privacies, intent on mating with the intangible inner being of fame. But only master photographers succeed. As testimony of the journalistic need to uncover something new, celebrities are over-interviewed on everything from bedtime readings to bathroom rituals. One can only assume this is what prompted Barbara Walters to ask Katharine Hepburn "What kind of tree are you?" Barbara attempted to rattle the uppermost branches of the Hepburn psyche to see what kind of fruit would fall, because celebrity should be about the person and not the larger-than-life media illusion. Serving this interest, *Private Dreams of Public People* lets the reader get into bed with the celebrity mind and nestle with its glittery, klieg-lit unconscious.

I had an intriguing curatorial concept. Why not gather dreams from dreamers of every discipline of the Arts, and from every form of celebrated notoriety, to learn if talents are protected, worried over or reflected upon within these dreams. I wondered if there was a link between dreamers and their professions or talents, and if dreams reflect their dreamer's life direction. The first celebrity dream I received suggested this was the case—Dr. M.T. Mehdi, peacemaker and former secretary general of the National Council for Islamic Affairs, dreamt of world concerns. I was encouraged to continue.

The more celebrity dreams I interpreted, the more similarities I found within specific artistic domains, such as the perennial actor's nightmare—being given the wrong script or forgetting one's lines—the professional's performance anxiety dream that never stops recurring. There were numerous dreams of musicians worried about losing their skills, artists worried about losing their paintings, and politicians fretting over their resourcefulness, or lack thereof. Indeed, many dreams corresponded with the personality and the role it plays in society. Before I interpreted G. Gordon Liddy's dream, I mulled over what sort of dream would lawlessly break into Liddy's mind in the middle of the night, after his having gone from chief security advisor for President Nixon, and thus guardian of the country, to being incarcerated. Mr. Liddy told me he dreamt he was under siege, protecting a woman who lived in a house of fifty rooms (the United States, perhaps). But who was this woman? Nixon?

Lots of questions needed answers. Do acquisitive moguls dream of money? Do architects dream of vertical mobility? Did Jacqueline Bouvier dream of becoming ensconced as an icon in the universal collective unconscious? Would the retired Kareem Abdul Jabbar dream of decadent athleticism? It was a mystery to me. I wondered what brainy dreamers dreamt; the ones who garnered perfect scores on their SATs. I found my answer when I interpreted the dream of technology's wunderkind, Esther Dyson, who used a computer's text search to escape from a tight spot in her evening reverie. Honestly, she did.

If experience is synonymous with history, then dreams are historical, and these dream portraits of celebrated beings are of historical significance. As history is passed on through the years, the unconscious records our personal histories over time, making dreams the standard bearers of our individual existence. If dreams—like genetics—are the by-products of our experiential heredity, dreams will resemble their dreamers. In other words, the house that Jack dreamt is indeed Jack himself. And we need neither Geary nor Gwathmey, Johnson nor Pei, as we are the lone architects of our dreams, striving to remember the overall design, the delicate blueprint of our construction—for unlike India's Taj Mahal, dream structures are not limestone, but vaporous like perfume. Dreaming is comparable to looking into a hall of mirrors at Versailles and seeing oneself angled from all sides: past, present and future. But this panoramic view evaporates too soon like breath on a mirror, taking with it our inner landscape, filled with the distinctive markings of conflict resolution, and the towering spires of wishful aspirations. This is why we dream in the dark—because fireworks cannot deliver their decorative potential in daylight. If dreaming is to illuminate it must be esthetically explosive, and unforgettable. We must ooh and aah from the magnitude of the voltage, thrash and recoil from the emotionality of the event.

Long before the hieroglyphic writing on the walls—and even before primitive speech—dreams were an ancient mode of envisioning expression, determining emotion and atmosphere. In fact, dreams may well have been the first theater. Strictly speaking, dreams are neither imaginary nor real, but a combination of what could be imagined as being real. This is the drama of the world of the unconscious. The velvet curtain opens, and inhabitants that slouch in the daylight boldly emerge like Pepe La Moco in the Kasbah, safe in their subterranean world. The real world is replaced with a staged production. Yet there is nothing linear about a dream. It is much more like Julian Beck's Living Theater, with audience participation at the most unexpected, haphazard moments. Dreaming has a theatrical bent that effects our senses through actions, intonations and the subtlety of gestures. The stage performance speaks to our inhibited selves of what we conceal from everyday experience. In short, dreams make an audience of the mind, and compel it to sit and look at the sources of its conflicts. The staging is the maneuvering of props within the visualized scene. The craft is the expression of ideas through the use of symbolism. The script—or narrative text—is the accoutrements of memory. As in theater, the lighting is directed, the focus intense, for the mind must be captivated, fascinated, and led to believe that a personal revelation is recoverable. The mind must unearth something cathartic for its viewers—its dreamers.

Whether or not my dream interpretations are a good narrative fit, the celebrity dreams in and of themselves display an intangible image that the medias cannot penetrate—for dreams have a way of presenting things *autrement*. With the depth of its reporting erased by the drama of its presentation, the media rarely presents more than the tangible, public self of celebrity. Yet within this book—composed of the simple, heartfelt things people dream of—both dreams and stars come out at night. As the reader will see, however sumptuous and richly textured the commentaries of celebrity lifestyles may be, the mind of the dreamer is infinitely more opulent.

It is well known that people with talent practice their skill five or six hours a day to hone it to perfection. What is not readily known is that dreaming is a talent, but even though we practice for hours each night, there is no competition to determine how well we have honed our skill. If remembered and interpreted, we bring dreams with us in all their voluptuousness wherever we go. More often than not, they pass by like speeding trains, leaving our forgetful minds only the faintest memory of their fugitive whistle. Because dreams are like tissue, they tear easily, and must be pinned down like butterflies before they flutter their beauty over a fragrant flower we will never smell again. We are that bloom, that elusive scent.

Yet we are all celebrities in our dreams, and by writing them down we can make them last and immortalize ourselves forever.

Lauren Lawrence

MICHAEL DOUGLAS

THE DREAM

"I dream I am visiting my father on the set. I wander off onto the set where everything is like a fantasy. I walk through all the activity, the film sets, the different actors. I walk past the animals, the props, and all the different rooms, the scenery and the settings and get lost in this world and become part of this world of fantasy, when suddenly my father finds me and shakes me on the shoulder saying it's time to go, and the dream abruptly stops."

THE ANALYSIS

Reviving a childhood experience awakens the original sense of excitement and wonder Michael felt when he first accompanied his father, Kirk, onto a Hollywood movie set. The "set" symbolizes the fantasy world of the father, and Kirk himself as an expanse of many different rooms the dreamer wishes to wander off into and explore. Whereas wandering off underscores Michael's self-reliant, adventurous spirit, getting lost or enveloped in his father's world reflects his wish for paternal identification.

The dream ends abruptly when Michael is hauled away from the fantasy world of the set where he is closest to his father. Thus, leaving the set essentially means leaving his father, but not before Kirk finds or symbolically discovers his son. Being told it's time to go is inspirational: Michael has the green light—he has permission to make the crossing into adulthood and into his father's world of fame and success.

JACQUELINE BOUVIER KENNEDY ONASSIS

THE DREAM

A fragment of a dream recollection as told to Jackie's stepbrother, Hugh D. Auchincloss III in the summer of 1950: "I dreamt we were in a castle, just after walking through the medieval walled town of Carcassonne in Southern France, when I imagined myself a grand heroine like Joan of Arc."

THE ANALYSIS

Symbolically, any form of domicile refers to the inner, walled-in private space within us and is considered a reflection of our personality—the more palatial the home, the grander the sense of self. Castles, therefore, represent a majestic presence, the remoteness of the personality and the wish for a protected, insulated existence. Detached from the mainstream of life, a castle signifies a sense of elevation and aloofness, and denotes a certain inaccessibility.

The ancient, medieval walled town of Carcassonne is Jacqueline putting up her own walls, protecting her personal space. There are thoughts of defending oneself from those who would climb over, from those invaders of privacy. Identifying with a martyr reveals Jacqueline's romantic nature and imaginative flair for the dramatic, her adventurous, loyal spirit, and innate sense of valor. It also reveals a profound gift of prophesy: as Jacqueline Kennedy she later inhabits a symbolic castle, The White House (code termed "Castle" in 1963 by the U.S. Secret Service Communications Agency), and becomes the ultimate martyr of the twentieth century. Interestingly, the future Mrs. Kennedy's dream is a prelude to the saintly Camelot era of her invention.

GAY TALESE

THE DREAM

"I recall a dream last night that centered around my going to a hotel. It seemed that my house was either under repair, or unavailable to me, perhaps because of some construction. I was alone, going to the Pierre Hotel [in New York]. I knew somebody who seemed to be in management—an engaging woman who I had some recognition of, and a great connection with, walked and walked with me through these inside corridors, and answered my questions along the way. I had no luggage. I followed her corridor after corridor, and I was never getting anywhere. I asked her, 'Where are we, The Waldorf?' Finally I wound up in another lobby, a second lobby where this room was. This room was in a corner of the lobby. I was dissatisfied. There were people around. And the bathroom was like those in Beijing—a primitive bathroom where people squat."

THE ANALYSIS

In that houses represent the person, a house under construction signifies that something is being built, shaped, assembled or revised—appropriate symbolism for an author in the midst of writing a book—for this is the narrative construction in progress. Leaving one's house indicates the wish for emotional distancing and objectivity. There is recognition of the engaging woman in management who fields questions and shows the dreamer the way, because she has done so before: as Talese's muse, she guides him again through the inside corridors of the imaginative unconscious. Although the path is circuitous, he remains on the ground floor, indicating the difficulties of the writing process.

   Without belongings—baggage—comes a keener sense of self-possession, and indicates a wish for detachment from the past. The lobby is the reception area symbolic of receiving and receptivity. The people that are around the room in the corner of the lobby represent an infringement of personal space—the intrusion of novelistic characters perhaps. Yet, as writers are observers, residing in the corner of the lobby affords Talese a view of all the action. The primitive bathroom that entails squatting alludes to staying grounded—and to roughing it out for a while.

JACKIE MASON

THE DREAM

"I run out of the house because it is on fire. I go into someone else's house to get away from the fire. A scantily clad young woman opens the door. I climb up some steps and tell her I am there to hide from the fire. But she knows me and wants me to tell her jokes. I do and she laughs so hard she cries."

THE ANALYSIS

As a house often symbolizes the mind, running out of the house signifies the wish to get away from one's thoughts. Fire symbolizes frenzied activity and movement. By fleeing fire—which produces smoke and sucks up oxygen—Jackie is literally trying to give himself some breathing space. This is the wish to slow down the pace of a very active mind, to find another house without a fire! But the new house contains fire of another kind—the flame of desire—in the form of a scantily clad young woman who opens her door. The open door of the female symbolizes the wish to be welcomed sexually. The young woman represents an escape from the mental to the physical realm, although, as we will see, Jackie's quick wit and clever quips can never be fully left behind, as they are required material.

The rhythmical act of climbing up steps represents sexual activity. A disguised sexual connotation is revealed when the young woman recognizes that the dreamer is a comedian. Asking him to tell jokes is euphemistic for wanting him to perform. Laughing so hard that she cries symbolizes sexual satisfaction, as tears are bodily secretions. This is the wish for an erotic conquest. The dream also reflects Jackie's desire to continue his life's work—perhaps at his own expense—presenting laughter to the world.

GEORGE PLIMPTON

THE DREAM

*"In my dream fragment there's going to be some
exam or test that I forget about."*

THE ANALYSIS

Plimpton has had what I call a caffeine dream: an anxiety provoking dream which serves up
a powerful stimulant that keeps dreamers on their toes. These examination dreams, however,
are often dreamt by perfectionists—by those least likely to be caught unprepared—and the
dream itself is a test, a trial run, a crisis situation that the dreamer must deal with. The dream
is an instructor shaking a finger at the dreamer to ensure that awareness is never lacking.
Self-expectations are high, and concerns are about meeting society's deadlines.

    The dream is confrontational, and represents self-critical, conscientious natures, and the
value placed on knowledge and awareness. The symbolic, subliminal self-reproach within the
dream comes from a fear of not being able to maintain a certain level of attainment—a self-
imposed standard of greatness. Such is the importance of vigorous preparation: Plimpton, who
has tried to do almost everything, wants to make sure that when he does it, he does it right.

SENATOR JOSEPH
LIEBERMAN

THE DREAM

*"I dream I am lying on the grass on a warm, sunny day, looking up at a tree above
me. All at once, the tree bursts into multi-colored blooms and then each blossom
opens into a multi-colored bird. It is like some animated fantasia, full of beauty
and fancy."*

THE ANALYSIS

Looking up at a tree tilts Senator Lieberman's dream in an optimistic direction as the tree
represents the tree of life, with all life stemming from the same seed in a continuity of spirit.
The multicolored blooms symbolize the wish for harmony in a nation of cultural and ethnic
diversity. The burgeoning blossoms signify that growth leads to developmental change, and is
revelatory—each blossom reveals an inner nature of transformation.

The dream is concerned with freedom of expression. The bird that emerges from the
bloom represents far-reaching ambition, and the fulfillment that comes from opening up and
evolving: what is fixed becomes mutable, and what is structurally set is able to fly away from
its roots. The animation of the dream images underscores the enthusiastic and exuberant nature
of the dreamer.

TESSA BENSON

THE DREAM

*"I was at my grandmother's house in Seguin, Texas. But it was before she got sick
and passed away. She looked young and I was young and we sat on my old rusted
green swing-set (that was broken ten years ago.) And I felt like I was a child again
and all that I wanted to do was go to the movies and water ski. And she was
putting my socks on for me, and wiping the dirt off my feet."*

THE ANALYSIS

In this love visitation dream there is the wish to recover the past and fix it in places where
it is broken. The deceased grandmother is young and healthy again, and the swing-set is
workable. Whereas the swing symbolizes the back and forth movement from present to
past, the swing-set signifies Tessa's wish to share the same space with her grandmother with
whom she is now *tête-à-tête*.

   Having socks put on represents Tessa's wish for protection from the elements, as her soul
(sole) will be kept clean. The symbolic action of wiping dirt off Tessa's feet exemplifies a way of
dealing with the muck we sometimes step in—as if the grandmother has said, "When you've got
some mud on you, give it time. Let it dry, and it will brush right off." The dirt that is wiped
away also signifies the dreamer's wish to leave the terra firma of the living momentarily behind
and reconnect with the loving ministrations of her deceased grandmother.

KURT VONNEGUT

THE DREAM

"Sometimes I dream that I murdered someone many, many years ago, and the police have only now found undeniable evidence that I was the one who did it."

THE ANALYSIS

Novelist Kurt Vonnegut's unconscious appears to have been the subject of investigative reporting, as the police—the superego—have found what they were looking for all along: undeniable evidence of his culpability. What was covered over has now been found; in Oedipal terms, a fading record of an ancient guilt perhaps or a validation of hostile impulses that were lain waste. As indictment is expressed without indignation, the wish is for self-recrimination. But because the dreamer is wanted, his wish is to be sought after.

What has been done away with—or murdered—is censorship or repression, in that Vonnegut's dream is one of conscience and responsibility. What was killed in the past is the former self, the old existence of the dreamer, which brings remorse. As death symbolizes finality, an irreversible abandonment or departure may have occurred. The passage of time encourages reflections about personal significance—in the long run all actions and choices are accounted for.

CHRIS KATTAN

THE DREAM

"In my recurrent childhood dream I am six years old. My mother has picked me up from Mt. Baldy, the school I used to attend up in the mountains. I get in the backseat of the car, which is parked in the middle of the road, when my mother says 'Hold on. I have to lock up the school.' As I watch my mother walk up to the school to lock it, I feel the car starting to move a little bit as if the brake was released, and then the car starts rolling forward heading downhill. I yell for my mom who is choosing keys, and hit the window to get her attention but she cannot hear me. She is too busy to notice me trying to get her attention."

THE ANALYSIS

Saturday Night Live comedic genius Chris Kattan's dream recalls the silent angst of Charlie Chaplin who made us laugh at the misfortunes and absurdities of life which are the basis of the comedic genre. His childhood separation anxiety dream is a wake-up call at a pivotal age when the wish for independence is often challenged by the fear of loss of love. The school that is being locked represents the nurturing mother, the teacher, the rule maker. Similarly, keys symbolize an entry point as well as an exit and the sense of abandonment; in the absence of his mother his life will go downhill. But the mother says "Hold on…" an affirmation that allows Chris to move along his way at his own speed and exhibit his driving force. This reflects the willful individualism of the dreamer.

 The dream recurs whenever Chris feels stuck in the middle of the road of indecisiveness when the pressure is on to move forward in his life. Sitting in the backseat reveals Kattan is driven. Feelings of loss of control are quelled by the craving for release. The wheels of accomplishment must roll to reach new levels. The symbolic wish to be noticed by his mother is a metaphor for the creative individual's need for an appreciative audience.
(Mr. Kattan, we will never tire of watching.)

JOAN COLLINS

THE DREAM

"I often dream that there is a young girl with me, around four or five years old. Sometimes she's left behind and I have to go get her."

THE ANALYSIS

No wonder this diva of *Dynasty* is a timeless beauty. Just look at her dream. The young girl who often accompanies Joan is the dreamer herself, tapping into a reservoir of kinetic energy and youthful exuberance. There is an effort not to be jaded by experience, or disconnected from one's inner child. Innocence must never be lost sight of, for there is the desire to look at things for the first time with fresh eyes—and to maintain an optimistic world view.

Watching over a child imbues the dream with an invigorating sense of purposefulness and responsibility. The dream is self-empowering as it envisions the best of both worlds: the wisdom of experience stays alongside the uncomplicated simplicity of youth.

MILOS FORMAN

THE DREAM

"I am standing in front of our little house in a small town called Caslav, with my hand on the doorknob. I hear the sweet voices of my mother, father and brothers talking inside. The house is surrounded by a garden, where not ten yards away from me, partly hidden in the bushes, a witch is hiding: a scraggy old creature with wild graying hair, long fingernails, a toothless mouth and dressed in dirty rags. Her hand signals me to step away from the door. I won't do that. I laugh at her, provoke her: come and get me. I feel safe with my hand on the door. Then, faster than I can open the door and reach the safety of the house, the witch grabs me and throws me into never ending space. I am falling and falling, passing indescribable surfaces that keep changing from smooth to rough. When the space is smooth I feel elated and happy. When the space is crumpled I cringe, suffer fear and feel utterly miserable."

THE ANALYSIS

Pleasurable feelings are transformed into painful anxieties in this recurrent childhood dream that contains a taboo fantasy common among small boys, where self-punishment is inflicted as a means of mitigating guilt. Partly hidden in the bushes the submerged sexual urges are making themselves known. The doorknob is a phallic symbol that empowers the small boy to feel brave enough to provoke the witch. But the boy is literally caught with his hand on the door (a symbol of a forbidden act) and punished accordingly by the witch, who sends him falling into never-ending space. Whereas dreams of falling represent the surrender to an erotic temptation, an endless unsupported fall reveals Forman's self-reliance and independence

Surfaces relate to the sense of touch, and feelings that arise from it. The smooth, extended falling space represents sexual activity with its indescribably pleasurable sensations. The crumpled space refers to sexual culmination—something has collapsed. This is why there is no longer elation but only cringing—a drawing back into oneself, which makes the dreamer feel utterly miserable.

Dreams of descending signify the search for a deeper self-knowledge. Similarly, dreams dealing with varying sensations, such as surfaces ranging from smooth to rough, suggest the evolving process of maturation. The witch is the dangerous force that unites the dreamer with his introspective sense: quite literally, she unearths his unconscious personality in the never-ending space, the depths he falls through.

LENA OLIN

THE DREAM

"Throughout my childhood I had this recurring dream that I would walk into this city all alone, and the city was empty. There were no people or cars on the street. I missed my dog. (In reality I had a dog that I loved passionately.) When I found my dog he would be lying there. The head would be intact but the body was missing; the skin was there, but not the skeleton. I would go and pick up my dog to pet him and it was like picking up a piece of cloth!"

THE ANALYSIS

In this coming of age dream, young Lena reveals her profound philosophical insights. There is already a sophisticated awareness of essence and being. The disembodied head of the dog symbolizes the wish to find the essence of things—to free the substance from the form.

The city is the dreamer herself, empty of the kind of identity that is molded through life experience. In other words, there is the realization that a child has much to soak up, learn and become. Similarly, the dreamer is also the dog—her own best friend—with her insides missing. As there is no interior, her persona has not yet fully formed. Without the skeletal framework, the rigid structure, the body is symbolically viewed as a cloth, an exterior which can be fashioned or sewn into different costumes and shapes. This creative idea is particularly fitting to a burgeoning actor who must receive and be transformed into new roles.

The emphasis on the head—which is intact—represents to Lena that reason and contemplation are of utmost importance.

FRANCESCO CLEMENTE

THE DREAM

"My mouth is open, my eyes cast down to the ground. I am climbing backwards a steep, precarious ladder. I don't find it strange that, as I climb higher toward the sky, the ground, covered in rubble, keeps getting closer and closer."

THE ANALYSIS

As an artist must stay connected to the physical world, Clemente, even in wishful ascent, keeps an eye on the earth, making sure it remains close. Thus, the wish to ascend is conflicted with the wish to climb back—or back up—toward where one came from. The open mouth represents the womb, poised to receive or issue forth. The downcast eyes mourn their separation from mother earth.

Moving skyward brings the dreamer nearer the ground, because the creative process elevates through its contact with the material world. Celestial footing is precarious, as the self has widespread, earthly roots... even in its rubble, its own debris.

There is an holistic idea of the circularity of time wherein the future curves back into the past, and the sky eventually becomes earth again. Like Escher, who played with perspective, the concepts of up and down, ascending and descending, are not clearly delineated but rather mysteriously left to the imagination. Things are artfully turned round, confounded and looked at in different ways; nothing is considered strange by the creative mind.

GORE VIDAL

THE DREAM

"I have a recurrent actor's nightmare where I am on stage and I have forgotten my lines, and I panic not knowing what script I am supposed to perform."

THE ANALYSIS

Performance anxiety dreams typically recur before some responsible action is expected of the dreamer—the daunting task of putting himself under the public spotlight. Caused by the fear of being caught off guard, these dreams of self-presentation represent a certain guardedness or conscientiousness, since they insure that the dreamers will be prepared for all eventualities. Thus, Vidal's recurring dream may be viewed as a line of defense. It is a reciprocal agreement wherein the unconscious shakes hands with consciousness to produce a desired result.

For both actor and writer, the script symbolizes the narrative. Not knowing what script to perform indicates the intellectual choice involved in communicating ideas. Viewing oneself on stage symbolizes the aesthetic elevation of the dreamer. There is the desire for a higher understanding as the dreamer wants to know what part he is to play in life.

THE DREAM

As told to Larry Geller (right), personal hairstylist, spiritual mentor and close friend of Elvis, at Graceland: "I had this dream that the Presley Brothers were performing. My twin brother Jesse and I were on stage, both wearing white jumpsuits with guitars slung around our shoulders. He was the spitting image of me except he could sing better."

THE ANALYSIS

It is not surprising that Elvis dreams of sharing the incredible phenomenon of his fame—even his talent—with his stillborn brother Jesse, in that losing a twin often produces survivor's guilt. What is interesting, however, is that Elvis endows his brother with a better singing voice than himself. This brings spiritual meaning to the dream as the brother's voice is coming from another place of heavenly timbre and resonance.

Teaming up with one who has passed to the other side reveals the wish to be elevated to a higher level of existence—within the dream this higher level is symbolized by the performance stage. The guitars around the shoulders are symbolic wings or angelic equipment as this is an angelic scene from above—singing voices, stringed instruments and the color white represent spiritual wisdom and purity. Taken literally, jumpsuits signify suits that jump, or rise. Thus, the dream underscores Elvis's spiritual quest: to become one with a heavenly being in the hope of joining his twin on the other side—whole and enlightened.

CANDACE BUSHNELL

THE DREAM

*"I keep having horrible nightmares that
blood is coming out of my mouth."*

THE ANALYSIS

In a reverie that should be titled "Bleeding Candace" what may seem gruesome is actually hot
and gutsy. Candace's dream is symbolically poignant in that she is a writer, for the blood that
trickles from her mouth is her life blood, or her essence spilling forth. This reveals that the
dreamer's fundamental nature is coming out through her mouth… and means that her writing is
pure and true, because it comes from the heart. The mouth—which parts like the Red Sea—is a
symbol of communication that represents the need to speak out. There is the tumultuous wish
to live life at its fullest. In that blood is tasted, Candace needs to savor life in its most elemental
form to fully experience it. Interestingly, as the color red is phonetically rendered as *read* the
dream is imbued with an urgency to communicate in a way that will be read or understood in
its deepest sense. In other words, Candace wishes that whatever comes out of her mouth will
be read (red).

In Freudian interpretation, anything that comes out from the body of a female is viewed
as symbolizing a conflicted or thwarted wish for pregnancy, as there is the need to fill a void. Yet,
as is often the case with writers, the concept of pregnancy is equated with the creative process.
Because this dream recurs, it indicates that Candace will never be drained of her creative juices.

GRAYDON CARTER

THE DREAM

"This dream I have, I've had since adolescence. And I still occasionally have it. I'm falling to earth. Not quickly, but rather slowly enough to take in everything that is approaching. I am headed toward a schoolyard in Europe I played in as a child. I am maybe fifty feet from the ground when I begin, out of desperation, to flap my arms. This slows my descent. I flap a little more vigorously and begin to achieve some lift. Pumping them harder still, I pull myself out of my dive and swoop low across the schoolyard and then up. The more I move my arms, the greater my success at doing turns and loops and zooming in just over the heads of my classmates. Just as I reach some level of joy in all of this, I wake up."

THE ANALYSIS

When a falling dream forms an alliance with one of flying, transformational skills are at work—Carter is able to turn feelings of desperation into some level of joyous success. Both dreams are involved in the process of liberation or letting go. But whereas falling dreams involve control issues and feelings of powerlessness, flying dreams empower dreamers with the sense of omnipotence. In other words, the one reveals the desire to be grounded, the other reveals that adolescent fears *are* groundless.

The symbols of self-mastery—the up and down movement of swoops, dives and loops (and this dream is pre-Harry Potter, mind you)—indicate Carter's innate faith in himself even when he is not on terra firma. For through his deft handling and personal maneuvers he will never hit bottom. Although his modesty precludes a lasting joy, perceiving himself over the heads of his classmates reveals Carter's strong self-image. And in light of his life accomplishment, this vanity is fair.

PATRICIA DUFF

THE DREAM

"I have this recurring dream that I am being engulfed by a huge tidal wave. I can either run through the water or dive under it, but it is difficult to move quickly through water, so I just sort of stand there in horror."

THE ANALYSIS

Dreams of being engulfed or enveloped usually refer to romantic involvements wherein one's partner is perceived as overbearing and possessive, manipulative and regulatory. Similarly, these dreams often indicate the sense of being overwhelmed by a powerful, unstoppable presence as one's personal space is being violated, or more correctly, infringed upon. There is an element of threat, of being swallowed up or subsumed by a force beyond one's control. Hence, these dreams call into question aspects of ownership since they represent the loss of one's freedom of choice and decision-making capabilities.

The tidal wave symbolizes a voluminous onslaught looking to subsume all in its path, or one who impinges upon another: a dictator or a territorial male who wants more land to annex and call his own, to affirm and extend his image. Perhaps Patricia's anxiety dream refers to a powerful ex-husband. The wish of the dream is to avoid an uprising by simply getting through the wave or beyond it—or to dive underneath it—to keep a low profile and avoid being the target of its wrath. Yet, on another level of interpretation, anything that comes out of the water—even a tidal wave—symbolizes rebirth and is often related to rescue fantasies and wishes of being swept away.

CHRISTOPHER BUCKLEY

THE DREAM

"There is this dream that sometimes troubles my sleep: I have somehow climbed to the top of a several-hundred-foot-high tree, with no branches, and having reached the top, it starts to sw-a-ay, and sway, and s-w-a-a-a-ay. It produces the most peculiar sensation in a somnolent stomach, and I am always keenly happy to awaken."

THE ANALYSIS

Having reached the summit of a tree with no branches to deviate from, there will be no risk-taking, as Christopher cannot go out on a limb. Yet it is hard to remain aloft, and harder still not to waver in deliberation. The swaying motion signifies indecisiveness, and the wish to consider one's options by weighing the alternatives. It is as if Christopher is on a scale where he himself is hanging in the balance.

Similarly, there is the wish to avoid being grounded, to inspirationally rise above or elevate one's point of view in the hope of broadening one's scope or perspective. The tree that teeters to and fro symbolizes a lack of rigidity—the lithe spirit of the dreamer that may bend but will never break.

WALLY SCHIRRA

THE DREAM

*"During my youth my best dream recurred frequently, where I would just
lift off from the ground and start flying in the sky. I would fly higher and
faster and farther than could be imagined. It was a wonderful dream of
mine that was accomplished in reality by the NASA space program.
Once I became an astronaut these dreams stopped. In space, I did not dream,
as I hardly slept. I had to fight to get to sleep because I was never physically
exhausted. Because without the weight of the body, movements don't take
any energy. Interestingly, the body fell into the fetal position."*

THE ANALYSIS

Indeed, flying dreams are the best dreams to have, as they empower the dreamer with superman
qualities and the sense of omnipotence. As flying is against the pull of gravity—against the basic
laws of nature—flying dreams are usually dreamt by independent thinkers, and by those who
take an optimistic view—who see all things as being possible. Thus, they signify the wish to gain
a broader perspective and be unencumbered by the restraints of everyday life.

These dreams represent the immense importance of one's personal space, and express the
high-minded wish for transcendence and unrestricted freedom. As dreams of self-empowerment,
it is no wonder that Mr. Schirra's dreams of flying stopped in 1959 during his actual flights into
space (which led to his becoming commander of Apollo 7's eleven-day flight in 1968), for the
awesome, heroic, emancipating wish of his dream—to break boundaries and fly faster, higher and
farther than imagined—had been fulfilled.

EMANUEL UNGARO

THE DREAM

"In my dream I am starting my next fashion show with the sound of voices as well as the music from the film Casablanca. *Then I hear the voices of Humphrey Bogart and Ingrid Bergman intertwined with the famous 'Play It Again, Sam'... All of that in the dark, just before the first girl [model] steps onto the runway."*

THE ANALYSIS

Ungaro's dream reveals his preoccupation with his life's work—the task of creating a dramatic statement through fashion. An inspirational tone is created within the dream; voices are heard and music is played. A theme is visualized for his upcoming fashion show: a timeless romantic drama tinged with a sliver of danger and intrigue. For Ungaro wishes to create a classic collection filled with visual drama and excitement, one as memorable as the movie classic *Casablanca*. The song title "Play It Again, Sam," symbolizes Ungaro's romantic nostalgia for another show, another collection, and his desire to replay past successes. It is a prelude to the song lyrics of "As Time Goes By," where fundamental rules still apply. Because the dream takes place in the dark, Ungaro creates internally from an imaginative, inner muse.

The most memorable scene of *Casablanca* takes place on an airport runway where Ingrid Bergman gives a final good-bye to Humphrey Bogart. Within Ungaro's dream, this scene is played out on another runway—the fashion show runway or catwalk—illustrating that Ungaro's world of fashion is symbolically intertwined with the romantic fantasy world of the movies.

Emanuel Ungaro wishes to note that his October '96 Prêt-à-Porter fashion show opened exactly as dreamt, and with much success, because he followed his dream.

HELENA BONHAM CARTER

THE DREAM

"As a child of about four or five I had a recurring dream. In the dream I am wandering down a sandy lane in a forest. It is very dark. Suddenly around six feet in front of me a mound appears, and out from this mound pops a crab. The crab started chasing me. I turned and went the other way, retracing my steps. At the top of the lane there was this huge gothic mansion, but between this sanctuary and me was this carpet of live snapping lobsters, and the crab was still behind me."

THE ANALYSIS

At a transitional phase of life, Helena travels a lonely road into the forest of repression with the intention of breaking from the dependent, restrictive lifestyle of a young child. But, like Little Red Riding Hood, her excursion into the woods—her daring quest for self-awareness—is met with opposition. Initiation dreams often pit dreamers against evil or frightening creatures that represent ordeals or trials of courage to be triumphed over. For these dreams are heroic attempts to illuminate and move the personality forward in its stage of development.

Wandering off alone indicates Helena's wish for independence. The forest primeval symbolizes the unconscious or the unknown. It is dark because there is need for clarification. But she can only go so far as her path is blocked—she has stumbled on an inner, subterranean world of confrontation, a world beneath the surface, which is why there are ocean dwellers: crabs and lobsters. The crab that pops out is the dreamer's willful tenacity.

Dreams of being chased often signify the need to affirm moral and ethical values, as the word "chased" has the phonetic rendering of *chaste*. The crab makes Helena retrace her steps—return to familiar ground—and the security of the home. But the wish is conflicted; the gothic mansion—perceived as a sanctuary—is barred from access. Once again, initiation dreams often present obstacles or impasses with something good waiting on the other side. Immobilized between a crab and a carpet of lobsters is like being caught between a rock and a hard place. Thus, the concealed wish of Helena's dream is to ascend—to rise above her fears—and gain an increased awareness in the process.

CARMEN

THE DREAM

"It is winter. I am sitting on a park bench with my father (who is deceased). There is a blanket around us, so we are not cold. My father tells me, 'You will be all right.'"

THE ANALYSIS

As a concert violinist Carmen's father would frequently leave home to perform, leaving Carmen to await their many wonderful walks in Central Park upon his return. By filling the park with the warmth of her father's presence, and the warmth of childhood memories, Carmen's dream reverses the chill and bareness of winter—the season of leaving—as the wish of the dream is to reunite with her deceased father and gain consolation from this reunion.

Even in winter there is warmth between father and daughter—a blanket is around them. The blanket represents security and comfort, and reflects the wish to be taken care of, covered and protected. As the blanket is another symbol for the father, Carmen is blanketed in love.

Sitting down means it is not yet time to go. Poignantly, being benched means not allowed to play—Carmen's way of making sure that her father will not leave her as he did in the past to play violin. The park bench offers the reassurance of that which is nailed down, solid and permanent, and symbolizes something that will always bear the weight that she carries.

FEDERICO FELLINI

THE DREAM

In a preceding dream, Fellini dreams he is the chief of an airport, in charge of passport control. He does not allow a strange, ancient, ill-smelling Chinese man dressed in rags to enter because he feels that this man will somehow disrupt his life, and this fear causes him to feel ashamed. At this point, he recalls that "The scene changes to a room flooded in great water where I, in a ringmaster's top hat and tailcoat, am forcing a large rodent to swim in desperate circles, urging it on with a whip." John Baxter, *Fellini* (New York: St. Martin's Press, 1993).

THE ANALYSIS

In the first dream a strange Chinese man's arrival at passport control is perceived as threatening. He is a foreign persona, the Jungian shadow presence that consciousness must acknowledge—an unknown part Fellini is fearful of accepting into his life. The Chinese man does not gain admittance because his arrival is viewed as a disruptive departure from Fellini's conventional existence. He is perceived as ill-smelling because Fellini smells a rat.

In the second dream, Fellini punishes himself for his fearful behavior in his former dream—he is both ringmaster in charge of the whip, and the large rodent made to swim in desperate circles. The ringmaster's tailcoat is a symbolic substitute for the rodent's tail. The circle symbol is the Jungian archetypal mandala—the sphere around which everything spins—and signifies Fellini's desperate wish for a contemplative self awareness of the inner personality.

Both dreams reveal Fellini's conscious need for control: order is sustained in his internal world by the regimentation of an airport chief and a circus ringmaster. The whipping motion symbolizes a forceful need to prod himself on—the performance must be ongoing, circular, without beginning or end. Poignantly, both dreams reveal that Fellini is clearly running the show.

PAUL McCARTNEY

THE DREAM

"'Yesterday'… It came in a dream unto me. Only the music. So I thought, that's a good tune. I wonder what that is. Dah-da-dah… And I had a piano by my bed… And I was sitting at my piano. Anyway, so I said, what is this tune? I blocked it out. Then I went to all of my friends, John first, George Martin, our producer. I said, what is this tune, dah-da-dah? They said, don't know, but it's good. I couldn't believe I had written it. I thought I'd heard it….it was so complete (in my dream). The words took a little longer, but the tune itself came just complete. Came just out of a dream. So you've got to believe in magic." (As told to Larry King, on CNN June 12, 2001.)

THE ANALYSIS

Discovery dreams are similar to problem-solving dreams, but where the latter involve settling situations, making decisions or correcting faulty ideas, discovery dreams actually make discoveries—some scientific, some philosophical, some inventive and some immensely artistic. Sir Paul McCartney's discovery dream of invention reveals the creativity of the unconscious (or the magic, as it puts it), the muse within and especially the muse within music.

Paul's dream reveals that inspirational energies never sleep at night, but rather come alive in the dark like fireworks of the imagination. His melodic dream—an unforgettable composition of tonal form (and one of the Beatles' biggest hits)—reveals his sensitivity to sound and melody. The dream expresses his fervent desire to compose, and his wish for self-expression through music. More than anything else, Paul's dream reveals how the unconscious mind works while we are sleeping, and how involved it remains in our everyday lives, our talents and our life's work.

LOLA MONTES SCHNABEL

THE DREAM

"My head is at the foot of an arena. Ahead, are several Irish girls with chubby faces and Betty Boop slicked hair. In a chorus line, they turn to me with one eye glaring hard (my self-portrait glare). The next shot is a white room with clinical chairs. The girls are in stirrups. Their crotches, moving like damp cloth towels covered in spray paint and iodine that froths and foams, drop eggplants to the floor that turn to baby fetuses, near a long swimming pool. Dozens of babies fall and sink into the pool. There are bubbles, and not enough time to retrieve them all to the pool's cement edge before they sink and drown."

THE ANALYSIS

Innovative filmmaker Lola Schnabel has dreamt what I call a movie dream—viewed in terms of shots as opposed to scenes—that she has titled "Disaster of the Living." In part, Lola's dream is a birth fantasy: the chubby-faced chorus line is the extended phallus lining up to make a field goal. An eye turns to her in the way one turns into something, in that she becomes, and is procreated. While glaringly self-critical, this defiant, singular eye (phonetically rendered as "I") symbolizes the importance of going solo, and underscores Lola's uniqueness.

But more important, Lola's dream is about the creative process, from its embryonic inspiration to the disastrous consequences of its being critiqued or examined, hence the sanitized white room replete with stirrups and clinical chairs. The eggplants imaginatively signify the planting of eggs, the fertilization which takes place in the uterine pool of the creative unconscious. The babies, or ideational conceptions, sink in symbolic representation of the heaviness, the casualties involved in the artistic experience. There is an exhaustive responsibility to retrieve bubbles—exhalations from the world of the unconscious—before they expire, these ephemeral insights into one's nature. Delving underwater symbolizes that Lola has depth.

THE DREAM

*"I had a glamorous dream last night. Marilyn was allowed
to come back [to earth] for one day, and she was going to be
at Town Hall and Paulette Goddard took me, she got the
tickets. Paulette was all in white, as usual, and you'd think
Marilyn would be, too, but she was wearing a green metallic
kind of dress and that was a beauty mistake because, with
the lighting on stage, the dress was throwing green light all
over her skin and Paulette kept elbowing me about that.
Everyone was asking Marilyn questions about how the
famous people in heaven were, and she would say, 'Oh, she's
beautiful!' 'Oh, he's fascinating!' And someone asked her,
'How're you?' and she said, 'I'm divine!' And the way she
said it got a laugh, but then she didn't have anything else to
say—about anything—and she began walking up and down
the aisles, really panicking and beginning to sweat, like she
didn't have any repertoire. And then someone screamed, 'Is
there a director in the house' and I felt she was looking at
me, pleading. And then suddenly we weren't in Town Hall.
The two of us—Marilyn and I—we were on First Avenue,
I think, in the back corner of a dumpy restaurant that she
said she used to go to a lot and I was taping her and trying
to get her to talk, asking her about the Kennedys and if they
really killed her and things like that, but she kept saying she
was saving it for her own book, and I got so upset with her,
I said, 'Look, Marilyn, you're only here for one day!
How can you do a book?' But she wouldn't spill any beans,
she just kept saying, 'I could tell you things that would curl
your hair.' But then she wouldn't. And then I looked at my
ticket stub from the Town Hall thing and it said,
'$1,000,000' and I didn't know how it could be that much
unless prices had really, really gone up, so I wanted to know
what year it was and I was trying to find a mirror to see
how old I looked so I could figure out what year this was
when a ticket could cost a million dollars and then the phone
rang and I woke up."*

ANDY WARHOL

THE ANALYSIS

In November 1975, Andy Warhol told his friend and diarist, Pat Hackett, a curious identity dream he'd had about Marilyn Monroe. The image of Marilyn symbolizes Andy in a way that vivifies how the unconscious internalizes conscious identifications. Even with green light on her skin, Marilyn is still in the limelight. At Town Hall (which almost sounds like Warhol) the questions Marilyn is asked are met with meaningless, terse retorts much in the same taciturn conversational style as Warhol's. Monroe's lack of repertoire causes panic and sweat and echoes Andy's personal desperation and his fear of creative depletion, of being dried up artistically.

Having no director in the house indicates that Andy is without direction. In search of answers he drills his intransigent muse Marilyn, who does not spoon-feed answers but rather inspires the right questions. In a symbol of reflection, Andy tries to find a mirror—this indicates that self-recognition is floundering. He wants to see how old he is, if he is passé. Yet the million-dollar ticket price is a self-affirmation of his personal value and star power. By looking into the future, Andy assures himself that he will remain on the scene—pandered to by the likes of Paulette Goddard who spends a fortune on him as her escort of choice.

SOPHIA LOREN

THE DREAM

"In the dream I am about 13 years old. It's early morning. I'm walking on a beautiful beach-side, enjoying the first sun rays, when a mountain-like wave grabs me, coming from the apparently calm ocean. I keep rolling and rolling in the furious water. I feel I'm dying... Suddenly the terrible water-wall drops, falls down. I resume walking like dancing toward the sun. The sun has become an enormous yellow globe. I feel very, very happy. And when I wake up I'm smiling."

THE ANALYSIS

Having just entered her teenage years, Sophia is in the dawn of her life, in a state of becoming. But while enjoying the sun rays, Sophia is already aware that darkness exists—the apparently calm ocean exterior in her dream hides a threatening inner undertow of danger. Although she is knocked down by forces beyond her control, she rises again, smiling, indicating her determined and optimistic outlook on life.

    Whereas water dreams are often birth fantasies, many have a spiritual nature, particularly those involving being immersed in, surrounded or embraced by water. For this is the religious symbolism of the baptism, and suggests a yearning for rapport with divinity. Sophia's rolling and rolling movement in the furious water resembles the action of getting cleansed in a washing machine, and makes her feel like she is dying. It is this wish for redemption and rebirth that brings about an abrupt transition from downfall to deliverance. The ever-present sun [son] that the released dreamer dances toward is symbolically viewed as the Savior, awakening immense happiness within the dreamer. Thus, Sophia emerges victorious from the darkness of despair into the light of hope, and responds to the chaos of the world feeling happy in the quiescence of her faith which reigns supreme.

THE DREAM

"A year or two ago I dreamt that I was on a safari adventure through the Amazon with 18 people. As we went on our journey people were being cut up by the natives or disappearing one by one, until I was the only one left. I entered a missionary-type town with a fountain in the center. I was surrounded by the natives that chopped up the other people. Then all the people that died started to emerge. They were standing in a circle around me. Then they said, 'Kelsey, you have to do what you've always done. Heal the children.'"

THE ANALYSIS

Venturing into the dense forest of the Amazon, Kelsey willfully enters the lush, hidden realm of his unconscious to confront all he has repressed. He is on a safari of self-discovery with himself as game: the hunted is in search of the hunter. What has not been stifled is his adventurous spirit.

The people being hacked by natives signify the need for emotional detachment, or a numbness of sensibility. Being the only one left—the lone survivor—indicates Kelsey's self reliance and expresses his emotional sovereignty. Those that are removed one by one from the scene represent the denial of affect, and the wish to forget painful memories of his past. Poignantly, Kelsey experienced the tragic dissolution of his family, and it is this sense of loss that is reflected within his dream.

The repressed unconscious, which tends to resurface, is symbolized by the metaphoric reemergence of the dead. The reemerged dead confirm continuance. Surrounded by those resurrected re-creates a wholeness that solidifies the preservation of the self. The narrative command "Heal the children" is Kelsey's coping strategy. A fragmented self image is viewed in its plurality. To this extent, the reemergence of the deceased makes Kelsey a part of all he is separated from, and all he has lost.

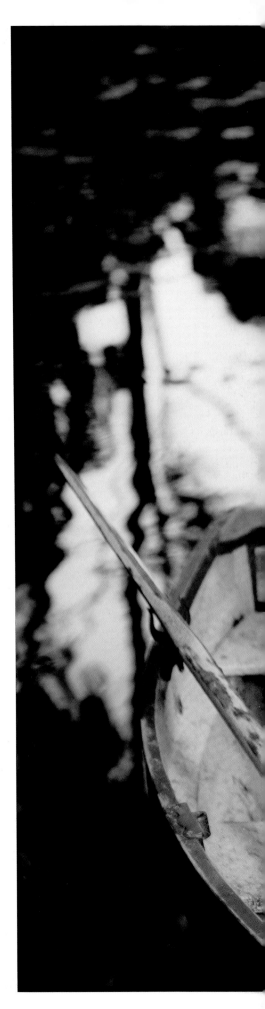

KELSEY GRAMMER

OLIVER STONE

THE DREAM

"I dreamt I was about to be executed in a bleak prison off the coast of California. They were preparing four or five of us for execution… a cluster of one woman and three or four men. We were to be killed one after the other in a warren of institutional-like rooms with windows looking out onto the ocean. It would be death by lethal injection. They were fitting us out for the execution with accoutrements… leather outfits, medically acclimated things that would make lethal injection easier. The concept of crossing over was unsettling to me. I saw this woman die first. Her body was shot through this coal shoot into the ocean. I saw these sharks with huge metallic tails like nuclear subs, circling around for their lunch. The warden, who was looking at his watch, had to get the executions over by 5:00 P.M. But they were puttering around, making bureaucratic screw ups. They couldn't get the vests on. It was very haphazard. The state could not make it work. They couldn't pull it off. I did not know if I would die today or not, if I would die by 5:00 P.M., if I would go to those sharks, and then I awake."

THE ANALYSIS

For a director of immense perfectionism, genius, creativity and productivity, the perfect execution of a project is prioritized. As such, Mr. Stone's dream assumes nightmarish proportions: instead of calling the shots, he passively endures watching another director—the warden—miss his deadline… the other executions. The mood is particularly bleak because deathly executions nullify the creative act, the birth of the artistic mind. The theme of being held captive, where the outcome is uncertain, reflects Mr. Stone's laboring over his screenplay-in-progress about prisoners of war.

What is unsettling is that dying is conceptualized as being problematic—screwed up by someone else's inadequacy. There is the disturbing Kevorkianic notion that our deaths are not our own, but rather dependent on the haphazard appurtenances of the state. Dying is symbolically viewed as a failure of the system. There is the fear of being tainted or infected by the lethal infusions of bureaucracy. Crossing over to the other side is viewed as the death of the individual self.

As "tail" has the phonetic rendering of *tale*, the huge shark tails serve as a grim reminder: they symbolize the tall stories of those in the industrial Hollywood complex who wish to consume—the sharks who hang around waiting to get fat from others by robbing them of their creative essence in the name of enterprise.

JULIETTE BINOCHE

THE DREAM

"I have often dreamt that I wake up within the dream."

THE ANALYSIS

Waking up in a dream symbolizes the willfulness of the dreamer to resist unconsciousness. In other words, submissiveness is never an option. Thus, even while asleep Juliette plays an active, revisionist role: she pulls back the taut reins of the nightmare, and gains control through self-monitoring. These are the dreams of natural born directors who must preside over all the shots. As awareness is valued, any retreat from reality is met with anxiety. Hence, there is watchful vigilance.

There is also the wish to awaken in the fullest sense, and reach a higher level of cognitive clarity, for dreams of awakening also signify the dawning of the self.

ANTHONY QUINN

THE DREAM

"I dream that I live on the edge of a placid lake. The house is not big enough.
Behind me is a big ruined stone castle. I am trying to buy it. But as I walk through
it I realize it is not practical for modern living as all the rooms are off a long, long
passage. But I am not happy living in the house while the ruined castle is behind me.
I love the view from that castle. I walk through both houses never at rest."

THE ANALYSIS

As legends often develop in medieval settings, the legendary Quinn has aptly dreamt of himself
in a castle. Whereas a placid lake symbolizes reflection and gives man a surface view of himself,
positioned on the edge of a lake suggests that Quinn is ready to take the plunge—to delve
beneath the depths of consciousness. Quinn is on the verge of self-discovery, (and in the midst of
divorcing his wife of many years!). As homes represent the dreamer's state of mind, a house not
big enough indicates a restrictive sense of being. But, in dreams, spatial relations also refer to
time—the stone castle offers an unalterable sense of permanence. The ruined stone castle (which
may refer to Mr. Quinn's estranged wife) is a fortification that has withstood the wrath of time.

    As the castle is situated behind the dreamer it symbolizes a landscape of the past that
beckons with its memories. Although the dreamer loves that wistful view, recapturing the past is
neither feasible, nor accessible, as all the rooms are off a long, long passage. Quinn desires the
remoteness and introspection the castle affords, but cannot give up the practicalities of modern
living. Walking through two houses, Quinn is split between two worlds—his past and his
present—and the different love relationships therein. And, like the ghost in *Hamlet*, Quinn walks
through both houses never at rest—a kingly spirit seeking an emotional resolution in his life
situation.

MADONNA

THE DREAM

*"I go to the doctor and she says, 'Oh, the fetal heartbeat is really weak.
I want to do an ultrasound,' and when she did, she said, 'The baby's dead.
You have pushed yourself too hard, and the baby's dead.' And I watch the
baby detach itself from the placenta and sort of float around in my stomach,
and I am sobbing hysterically, thinking 'I've killed my baby, My God, I've
killed my baby.'"* (Vogue, November '96).

THE ANALYSIS

Dreams of expectant mothers are often filled with anxiety over the well-being of their babies,
and, as such, this is a common anxiety dream. What is interesting, however, is that Madonna
remembers dialogue important in understanding the dream's true meaning. It is Madonna as
doctor who makes the harsh prognosis "the baby's dead"—for the baby is Madonna lamenting
the lost child of her own youth. It is the sad pronouncement that Madonna is baby no longer,
for the role of motherhood alters one's lifestyle, as it is a selfless position that requires endless
patience. With a change in self-image, the caretaker can no longer be footloose and fancy free.
Indeed, Madonna seems to have pushed herself into this pregnancy prematurely, as her dream
reveals a "what have I done?" attitude—Madonna sobs hysterically not only for the loss of her
childhood but in self-recrimination.

Watching the baby detach itself from the placenta reveals that the baby is not merely
viewed as an extension of the parent. The detachment symbolizes the non-symbiotic nature
of the mother-to-be. Madonna does not wish to control or manipulate as a parent, but will allow
her child the freedom and space it needs to develop an independent spirit. Importantly,
the dream reveals Madonna's conscientious nature—she is already watching her baby with
motherly concern.

CHRISTIAN LACROIX

THE DREAM

"As a child I often dreamt of going along a steep road, struggling uphill. The surrounding air was like at dawn or dusk: suffused with pink which made me think of candy. I knew that at the horizon behind the hill was a paradisiacal city, full of happiness, different architectures, colors and the most ideal pleasures. But I would always wake up before reaching it or within seconds of discovering it after finally arriving at the top."

THE ANALYSIS

In this recurrent initiatory, coming-of-age dream, Lacroix's struggle along the steep road symbolizes his wish for maturation during this transitional, twilight period in his life where the journey is of greater importance than the destination. It is neither dawn nor dusk, neither here nor there, as nothing has been fully formed or finalized. This is symbolic of the creative métier in flux and in a state of becoming. It is interesting to note that the young dreamer's senses are highly evolved and differentiated, particularly his visual awareness and his esthetic sense of color, shade and light, as this attribute is essential to his future success as a fashion designer.

Lacroix's intuitive knowledge of a paradisiacal city beyond view symbolizes his wish to ascend to the pinnacle of creativity within himself and experience the pleasures of the creative act. Regarding ascension, in an exquisite simile, the pink light of dawn is compared to candy, meaning that the glories of life are to be tasted and savored.

CYNDI LAUPER

THE DREAM

"I was around other women who were about to give birth and I was very pregnant. The women around me went into labor and had multiple births. But when I went into labor I gave birth to Mr. Bill. When I tried again I gave birth to Gumby. There was a woman next to me assisting me telling me that I wasn't ready yet and this was a relief, obviously, because who the heck would want to give birth to a Mr. Bill or Gumby for that matter."

THE ANALYSIS

Cyndi had this anxiety dream after she came home from her first class of the Bradley Method of birthing techniques where the teacher had been demonstrating the birth method with a doll. It is not unusual, therefore, that Cyndi dreamt that she gave birth to a doll. However, because dolls represent that which is make-believe, it should not be overlooked that they offer solace in that they eliminate the fears and worries of having to deal with the needs of a real live baby.

Since expectant mothers are often anxious over the well-being of their babies they often dream of their preparedness, or lack thereof, to assume the responsible role of caretaker. Cyndi reassures herself that she will be able to cope with the rigorous demands of motherhood by visualizing other women effortlessly and successfully having multiple births, but is self-critical at the same time—calling into question her own capability as all she begets are dolls. Because dolls like Gumby are made of soft, pliable, stretchy clay they are safe to handle, and most importantly they are unbreakable and immortal. This is the wish that Cyndi's baby will be hardy and indestructible. Cyndi may doubt that she is mature enough for the mothering experience, or ready to give up being a child herself as she is still playing with dolls. This inevitably reveals the sincere motherly concern of the dreamer who has been diligently practicing her lessons, even in sleep, to make sure—in a literal sense—that everything comes out all right.

THE DREAM

"I have this recurring dream where I am high diving off a cliff—so much higher than any cliff imaginable. I am scared. I have this falling sensation. It never resolves itself."

PETER BEARD

KODAK TRI X PAN

474 -7

SAFE

AK TRI X PAN

THE ANALYSIS

Falling is a liberating sensation. All about letting go, it shakes the dreamer free from guardedness and from the fetters of a preconditioned future. In that falling symbolizes the opening of a clenched fist—and loosening one's grasp—it is expansive and extroverted. With no support and no physical attachment, Beard's wish is for detachment and independence. No longer on familiar ground, the dreamer is out of his element, plummeting through the depths of existence where nothing is accounted for. There is a movement away from the concrete stabilities of life toward the abstract uncertainties; a leap of faith into the airy hands of the intangible, into a Yeatsian widening gyre where the center cannot hold. All for the better, because falling dreams establish trust in oneself and in one's survival, as one never hits bottom.

Initiating his downward spiral signifies that Beard surrenders to impulses regardless of consequences. Neither suicidal nor escapist, diving from the heights indicates the humility of the dreamer who is uncomfortable on top. Yet, the dream may also reflect something that Peter has given up in his life—something he has let fall by the wayside.

KATE MOSS

THE DREAM

"I dreamt I was in a fishing village walking up from the shore toward an old school friend of mine who I hadn't seen for ages. The school friend was now a fisher-lady. I went into my friend's house and there was a baby. The baby was hovering in the air over a plate of Heinz spaghetti. Below the baby some subtitles appeared saying 'Please let me get my spaghetti.' The baby was trying to grab the spaghetti, but suddenly it flew over to the corner of the room and stayed hovering there. Then I went to open the front door and I dropped my ice cream all over the floor. I said it was the baby's fault. When I awoke from the dream I felt euphoric."

THE ANALYSIS

In a scene reminiscent of a Louis Carroll storybook, Kate finds herself in Wonderland contemplating the strangeness of her own dream, which is why she has cleverly placed subtitles below the visual to facilitate her dream's translation. For what is dream interpretation other than a translation of symbols and images into meaningful ideas that can be understood during consciousness? As we shall see, dreaming of a fishing village represents the wish to fish, to reel in what is hidden beneath the surface. And with Kate as the fisher-lady fishing to pull up her past, it is not by chance that a baby rises over a plate of spaghetti and is subtitled. This communicates Kate's willful determination to understand her dream's poignant message: the hovering baby is Kate. Her wish is never to be grounded.

Yet there is also food for thought. Heinz spaghetti symbolizes canned or stored material from our past made of the numerous strands of memories we need to unscramble and unravel in our dreams. This unconscious material is symbolized as food, because it is intellectually nourishing, and inedible, because it is difficult to digest.

On another level, the hovering baby is also a manifestation of Kate's dream creation. Having left the ground, it resists being kept down or repressed, and reflects the persistent vivacity and lightheartedness of the dreamer. The open door symbolizes a wish for illumination as it ushers in the breeziness of a free spirit. Upon awakening, no wonder Kate is euphoric, for in a brilliant way she has broken free from gravity and is elevated. She is fly.

MARTIN LUTHER KING

THE DREAM

On January 15, 1968, at his 39th birthday party, King told his aide, Dorothy Cotton, a dream he had dreamt the night before: "I had died and no one was there. I yelled to Ralph [Abernathy], 'Ralph, bring those people standing there over here.'" (The History Channel, July 1999).

THE ANALYSIS

Less than three months before his tragic murder, Martin Luther King Jr. dreamt a prophetic dream that both prophesied his death and revealed his great humility. Having no one at his funeral reflects the humility of the great leader, yet also symbolizes the wish that his people do not grieve. Perhaps there is an inner understanding that his death will effect a positive change and bring about racial equality. The dream's sense of loneliness comes from King's leadership—to lead means that thousands are behind you but not necessarily with you.

The second part of his dream reveals King's desire to have his people attain in life what he has been granted in death—the promised land. In commanding his friend Ralph to bring his followers over, King reveals his wish for Ralph to continue in his stead to bring his people to a higher level, where they shall overcome.

HARRY BENSON

THE DREAM

"In my dream I am at a racetrack and I'm taking pictures. I look up about 200 feet and four people are near the edge of the roof of a building. I look down and then up again and see a man throwing himself into the crowd below. There is a terrible thud that actually wakes me up. (Perhaps the thud was my dog jumping off the bed, I don't know, but I heard a thud.)

THE ANALYSIS

When one of the world's great photographers dreams he is at the race track there is only one thing he is after... a photo finish of course! Even during sleep Benson is immersed in his métier—taking pictures.

In that sight is wedded to photography, the act of looking is prominent within the dream. The man who plummets into the crowd is the shot Harry is looking to photograph, or perhaps it is the dreamer jumping into one of his pictures. What is certain is that Harry is embroiled in the thick of things, capturing the moment. The thud that is heard is the wish to make an impact. The perpetual motion of looking up and down symbolizes the blink of an eye, but also the click of a shutter, and signifies the strong bond between Harry and his camera.

JAMES KING

THE DREAM

"Just before going off to shoot Pearl Harbor *with Ben Affleck I dreamt that
I showed up on set and… Oh my God… I couldn't remember any of my lines.
I was completely unprepared. I had to walk on set to do this scene with a famous
actor in a diner at a table and I couldn't remember my lines."*

THE ANALYSIS

Supermodel/actress James King has had a typical performance anxiety dream. These dreams
normally occur before an important event where something is expected of the dreamer, and are
often dreamt by perfectionists who demand the most from themselves. Viewed as such, the
dream serves as a final run-through in preparedness. By presenting the worst scenario of
forgetting one's lines, the accompanying dread and horror experienced in the dream is enough to
ensure that forgetfulness will not occur in reality.

     Dreaming of doing a scene at a table in a diner signifies the need for nourishment. The
wish to feed off the famous actor, to absorb and digest all he has to offer, is viewed as a measure
of James's hunger—her craving to be a great actress. The diner, as a symbol of basic homespun
food, represents King's desire to keep it real. No soufflés or crèmes brûlées here. She would
rather be down-to-earth than pretentious.

DEWI SUKARNO

THE DREAM

"I am standing inside my house speaking with my mother. I am complaining to her, 'You are so naughty. You are hiding yourself from me. You have made me so sad but you are not really dead, you are alive.' I hug her in happiness. But on the fortieth night when I hug her she is so soft and so light like a gem. Her body collapsed like a balloon without any air. There was nobody—nothing in my arms, and I screamed from fear."

THE ANALYSIS

On the eve of her mother's death, the former First Lady of Indonesia dreamt a visitation dream that recurred for forty consecutive nights. Her dreams conform to the Buddhist and Christian beliefs that departed souls remain earthbound for forty days. Defying psychoanalytic interpretation, Dewi's dreams must be viewed as a spiritual, mystical experience beyond scientific reasoning.

As death is seen as an abandonment, and even a betrayal, from an emotional perspective, Sukarno's admission of sadness, complaining and chastising, reveals her anger over the death of a loved one. A protective denial kicks in wherein the dreamer would rather think that her mother is naughtily or mischievously hiding than come to grips with the reality of her deathly absence. Dewi hugs her mother desiring to solidify the immaterial again, and to regain physical contact. And for thirty-nine days the dreamer is consoled by the nocturnal presence of her deceased mother.

On the fortieth day, reality and acceptance sink in and the bubble bursts. There is the sad realization that no more visitations will occur, which is why her mother's body collapses like a balloon that has lost all its air (the breath of life). The illusion, soft and light, is entirely perishable. The phrase, "There was nobody" is taken literally to mean there was no body—no earthly substance or form. Dewi screams because there is nothing in her arms, nothing left to hold onto. This signifies that a spiritual acceptance has occurred, Dewi has let her mother pass into the light.

CAMERON

THE DREAM

"I often dream I can never seem to run very fast or run away from situations or people. It suddenly all becomes slow motion (like walking through water) when I try to run."

THE ANALYSIS

Even a simple dream fragment like the one above is a complex way of looking at things. As an anxiety dream, and, in a sense, a dream of inhibition, the dream reveals motives for resistance or reluctance on the part of the dreamer. The dream represents the conflict between movement and stasis where an unresolved choice sometimes renders one motionless. Cameron may seek this powerless condition, as it forestalls decision-making. In simpler terms, Cameron may not be able to say no.

Restrictions are placed by individuals on themselves as a measure of precaution, or for the purpose of buying time. Cameron wants to run, but is thwarted by his own body, by the unwillingness of his legs to move effortlessly. This represents a mind/body split. A mental demand is being challenged by a physical need. This is reminiscent of a classic scene from *Seinfeld* that depicts Jerry's brain playing his penis in a game of chess. Cameron is in stalemate.

IVANA TRUMP

THE DREAM

"I had a dream that I was competing in the winter Olympics and had hit the slopes at 100 miles an hour leaving the rest of the skiers, many of whom I had known from the Czech team, far behind. I was completely alone on the slopes and felt free as a bird, soaring through the air without a care in the world and, of course, knowing that I had won the gold medal. When I reached the finish line the only spectators there were my three children. They were clapping and shouting, 'Mom, you're a winner! Mom, you're a winner! Mom, you're a winner!' I was suddenly awakened by my three young children and two dogs who had run into my bedroom at some unearthly hour in the morning and were jumping on my bed. To me this was better than any gold medal!"

THE ANALYSIS

Whereas emotions usually sink to the lows of the valleys after a divorce, Ivana's optimistic unconscious positions itself on the peak. Initially, dreaming of being atop a mountain may be viewed as the result of hard and arduous work and symbolizes a measure of achievement. Yet this position of prominence is difficult to maintain; on the steep slopes of life Ivana must watch out for the pitfalls, the ruts or mogols (especially moguls) along the way that may trip her up and bring her down. Leaving the rest of the skiers far behind reveals Ivana's independent spirit and sense of self worth—she is as comfortable breaking away from the crowd as from a highly publicized marriage. Not only can she make it on her own, she is a trendsetter as she leaves tracks behind for others to follow.

Hitting the slopes at 100 miles an hour signifies passionate determination—the fast pace underscores Trump's drive and ambition. In terms of personal fulfillment, Ivana's unconscious is already aware that she is a winner in the long run, as the gold medal that is won is the mother of all medals. The real prize is not lost sight of—her children are by her side, cheering her on.

MARIO BUATTA

THE DREAM

"Ever since September 11th, I have had this recurring nightmare. The city is being attacked again, and the buildings are shattered. Bombs are going off, and insects are flying all over… these huge water bugs, and I awaken horrified."

THE ANALYSIS

When two significant buildings—the WTC twin towers—pancake downward before our very eyes and leave in their stead a hideous rubble of pulverized dust, significant psychic trauma also remains. Buildings are structural edifices that symbolize the solvency of the self, and their destruction triggers feelings of inward dissolution, powerlessness and a sense of void. It is not unusual therefore to experience nightmares that evoke the emotional horrors of instability and fear.

A city is perceived as a womb symbol in that we live in it. Thus, a shattered city signifies that one's sense of protection, insulation and security has been compromised. The uncertainty of the moment leads to feelings of helplessness and despair. The bombs symbolize the impact to the psyche. The city under attack is viewed as an affront to the personality. For Buatta, a world renowned interior designer whose livelihood is based on creating beautiful interiors, the destruction of exterior façades is particularly threatening as it is viewed as an assault on the aesthetic sense. Internalizing this tragic event indicates Buatta's sensitivity and strong identification with the most powerful city in the world.

DIANE VON FURSTENBERG

THE DREAM

"I am looking at an Egyptian temple with no roof. All the people I ever knew are making this temple. All the people are adding to it. I am looking at this, very contented."

THE ANALYSIS

As a building symbolizes the self by housing the individual, an Egyptian temple represents a majestic and exotic sense of presence. Roofless, the temple affords an optimistic view—Diane can elevate as high as she wants without restriction—for the sky's the limit. The temple with no roof further reveals Diane's open-mindedness and accessibility, and underscores her free, liberated spirit, which is why she is content looking at this work in progress. The visual impression of the dream is that something is taking shape, something is in the making. Nothing is static because the dreamer is evolving.

The dream reveals that the building blocks of life are based on companionship. The friends and family making additions to the temple signify the importance of reinforcement gained through social interaction. The social aspect is what solidifies structure, and is the architect of Diane's life. The building process represents creative impulses. This build-up is also a commendation of sorts—a self-affirmation which reflects Von Furstenberg's constructive outlook. Diane wishes to leave some structure behind that will stand the test of time.

121

LYNN FORESTER
LADY ROTHSCHILD

THE DREAM

"I remember a dream where I am at the Columbia Law School library studying late into the night. There are stacks of books and coffee. The exam is the next day. And then I'm running and running and somehow I don't get to the exam, and I don't graduate."

THE ANALYSIS

I have often referred to dreams with missed examination motifs as caffeine dreams because they act as powerful stimulants that keep dreamers on their toes and ready for action. Lynn's dream has thankfully supplied the coffee as proof. The stacks of books and the coffee are symbolic equations—indicators of her love of stimulation.

Self-deprecating in nature, these anxiety dreams are the trial runs of conscientious individuals—tireless perfectionists eager for their wake-up calls. The shock value of missing an exam insures against being unprepared and highlights the importance of vigilance during wakefulness. In Lynn's dream, the process of studying that continues during sleep suggests it is valued more than the examination itself, which is never taken. Thus, the process or journey is more important than the destination—the final exam. Similarly, on some level, the graduating event may represent an undesirable finality or ending, which is why it is avoided.

TYSON BECKFORD

THE DREAM

"From time to time I have had dreams where I am playing basketball. I am going up for jump shots and trying to perfect my jump shots and slam dunks."

THE ANALYSIS

Dreams in which dreamers are actively involved in playing a sport usually indicate the strong physicality of the dreamer. Jumping, slamming, dunking… from the catwalk to the court Tyson is in motion working up a sweat, determined to perfect what he wants to excel in. And with the ball in Tyson's court he will make those slam dunks, for he is playing the game of life to win.

Almost all male dreams of putting a ball in a hole usually have sexual significance, and in this sport Tyson clearly wants to score. Yet, Tyson's dream is more about joyous self-expression, for the act of jumping up signifies optimism and his innate sense of happiness.

PATRICK DEMARCHELIER

THE DREAM

"In my dream I am running to my friends. I put my arms out like a bird and poof... I take off. My friends are watching. I fly around. Not very high, but high enough. It is a good feeling."

THE ANALYSIS

Flying dreams are dreams of self-empowerment, as they endow the dreamer with superhuman qualities and the sense of omnipotence. Revealing the need for independence and personal freedom, these dreams are the domain of free-thinkers in defiance of the rules imposed by the world. There is the wish for a lightness of being. Flying dreams in men, however, are often attached to sexual excitation because in the act of flying something rises up against the pull of gravity.

Although running toward friends suggests congeniality, rising above them signifies aloofness and the wish for detachment, to remove oneself from established ways of thinking. There is the need for personal space and to be unencumbered by societal restraints. Having an overhead view broadens the perspective and allows photographer Demarchelier to take in the whole picture. The act of taking off—moving beyond the surface—brings clarity and symbolizes Patrick's desire to strip away artifice. Poof! There is magic in the dream, similar to the photographic image that emerges from invisibility, as if to say that all things are possible.

INDIA JANE BIRLEY

THE DREAM

"When I was in India I had writer's block and I had this dream at that particular time: there was an empty white plate in front of me. It filled my entire vision… it was the entire picture. I broke it. I smashed it up."

THE ANALYSIS

The plate within the artist's nightmare literally serves up a platter of emptiness or blankness similar to a tabula rasa. In this way the empty plate, as a carrier of nourishment, symbolizes purposelessness and reveals India's momentary anxiety over lack of artistic inspiration—there is nothing on it she may use. Emptiness fills the entire dream landscape much as the mind of one with writer's block. The largeness of the empty plate consumes the entire dream picture and blocks all else. For a figurative painter, an empty plate is like an expressionless face; the lack of detail, like a blank canvas.

The color white signifies the absence of color, and with it the absence of the imaginative motivation. There is the fear of losing one's creative sensibilities. But the plate is broken and smashed in an attempt to rid the artist of the writer's block she is experiencing. Breaking the plate symbolizes India's willful determination to effectively end her dream, and gives her something to imaginatively piece together. The dream wish of India, niece of Maxime de la Falaise, is for transformation from an uninspired state to one of vitality where things shatter and come free of their static form.

HELENA CHRISTENSEN

THE DREAM

"I dreamt that I was with Hitler in a bunker in the last moments of his life as he was about to die. We were lovers. I was his mistress. He knew he was losing the war and wanted us both to die taking poison. He wanted me to do it first but even in my dream I knew I had to make him take the poison before me. I saw him die, and then I seemed to transport myself ahead to 1995, the time of the dream."

THE ANALYSIS

Übermodel/photographer Helena has dreamt a feminist's dream of self-empowerment wherein the wish to be released from male domination in its most heinous form is immensely strong. Hitler symbolizes the masculine ethos at its territorial worst, with the manic need to rule, order, control, manipulate and feed off the dehumanization of others. By convincing the dictator to die first, Helena proves she is above male victimization. This underscores the willfulness of the dreamer and her strong sense of self worth.

Helena's dream also visualizes a powerful anti-war sentiment: Make Love Not War, and reinforces the idea that the positivism of love eliminates negative forces in the world. As Hitler is the symbolic embodiment of hate, loving him makes hate succumb in its underground bunker. At the core of the dream is the fearful recognition of the dark side of humanity, a fear that is embraced. For only by embracing what is feared can Helena overcome or nullify the fear itself. If redemption is to follow, Helena must witness the death of evil as symbolized by Hitler. Once this is achieved, a transformation or rebirth occurs; Helena is transported into the light of a new era.

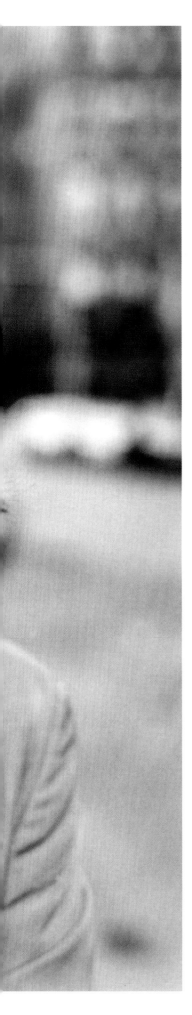

THE DREAM

"This is a dream I still remember from my early twenties. I am wearing a pea coat, carrying a duffle bag. I've joined the merchant marines. I'm showing my girlfriend, an achingly beautiful creature who makes a one time only appearance in this dream, my quarters, where I will spend the next three years. My cell is next to the engine room, so deep in the bowels of the ship that there is no window. I'm saying good-bye to my girlfriend: I'm hugging this girl tightly with grief and disbelief that I would volunteer for a job that would keep me from ever seeing her again. I wake up and my pillow is drenched in tears."

THE ANALYSIS

Dunne's coming-of-age dream has him going off to sea in a difficult journey of self-exploration. Possessions are minimal; only what fits in a duffle bag. This is a dream of letting go and of doing without, a dream of sacrifice wherein something in the dreamer's life must be abandoned. But, as predetermined abandonment necessitates feelings of remorse, the dream doles out its punishment—Dunne is confined to a windowless cell. There is a sense of decisiveness because without windows there is no reflection—and no way out.

    The dream has a conscience: feelings of guilt or regret are represented through grieving and self-recrimination. Yet the ship signifies embarking on a new life: the old self is enclosed deep in the bowels of the ship—the old existence in poignant, symbolic closure. There is sad recognition of the finality of endings. Perhaps the tears are for the death of dependence, as the dreamer must go it alone. This signifies the wish for autonomy and independence. Yet this wish is conflicted as the dreamer holes up in a womb-like chamber near the heat of the engine—the power source. The loved one is made to achingly witness or validate all Dunne is voluntarily giving up and is there for moral support.

MIGUEL FERRER

THE DREAM

"During my childhood I had a recurrent flying dream, but mine had a twist…I had to put on my swim fins first, and then I could tread the air as I would water. I'm be in my bedroom in The Dakota in New York City, sitting on the side of my bed, and I just start kicking. I push through my window and move out across the roof of the house, and then I go everywhere with a feeling of complete freedom… anything goes. It is joyous, celebratory."

THE ANALYSIS

As flying defies gravity, Ferrer's dream represents levity. There is the celebratory wish to emerge from the sheltered, dependent, interior world of a child. Flying beyond the home symbolizes independence, and the wish to fearlessly approach the outside world. The elevated status symbolizes the maturational ascent from adolescence to manhood.

But, Miguel's flying dream is non-traditional, non-conformist, even a bit flippant, as it imaginatively combines elements of swimming. In a cross between Superman and Flipper, the fin-wearing dreamer treads through the air and survives; in other words, he keeps his head above water. A submerged sense of self rises buoyant from the depths, and finds freedom of expression. The kicking movement represents the wish for confrontation; the forward thrust of the leg symbolizes a mind that does not look back at the past.

CAROLYNE ROEHM

THE DREAM

*"I walk over this hill and look down into a low valley.
I walked down into it where there is this glorious glowing blue
light. There is the serenity of a nativity scene… white colors,
blue colors, I think how beautiful all this color is."*

THE ANALYSIS

Whereas walking up a hill represents the arduous path
to the top, walking over the hill means the dreamer has
already been there—having surmounted an obstacle or
impediment en route. Roehm has traveled the road to
personal achievement and gone beyond. She descends
into a low valley yearning for depth or understanding.
The valley is the immense recessed landscape of the
unconscious where the instincts emit glowing light.
Walking into the blue symbolizes the wish to explore
unknown regions that require courage and daring.

The low valley is a depression she must
investigate. But Roehm's positivist's dream shuns
remorse, the downcast eyes, the descent, the solitary
foray into a hollowed landscape infused with blues.
Aware that sadness is only a place in time, Roehm
makes it a glowing place, and vivifies the moment.
The luminous nativity scene is self-referential of an
inner flame of renewal and rebirth.

Something has awakened within the dreamer's
unconscious. She has seen the light! In that color
represents emotions (blue symbolizes sorrow and truth,
and is also interpreted phonetically as "blew," signifying
a blown chance), Carolyne has the illuminating
revelation that feeling is beautiful, no matter what
the feeling brings.

THE DREAM

"In reality, I have five big studios. But in a recurring nightmare "I get to my studio and I don't see any of my paintings. House painters are painting the walls. I ask them what they are doing, and where are my paintings. They say the paintings were sold and now this is a shop, an office, or a company. They don't really know."

THE ANALYSIS

As one of the great painters of the twentieth century, Botero dreams a typical artist's nightmare—there is anxiety over protecting and maintaining his artistic talent, and the product of that talent. The studio is a representation of the painter himself: walls that are painted, or covered over, symbolize Botero's fear that the depth of his genius will be replaced by surface veneer, originality substituted for the house painters' uniformity. The phrase "I don't see any of my paintings" indicates that Botero's paintings are not seen but rather envisioned, and that the artistic process comes from within the unconscious.

Dreaming of sold paintings symbolizes separation anxiety from his work—all Botero is left with are bare walls. Botero, as the inspirational part of each canvas, has been robbed of his essence. Mystified, he wants to know the derivation of the wondrous creative spirit. As no one really knows where it comes from, no one knows where it will go.

FERNANDO BOTERO

PRINCESS MARIE-CHANTAL OF GREECE

THE DREAM

"When I was eighteen, one weekend I was staying over with my sister. I was on the bed in the bedroom of my parents' apartment at the Carlyle with my younger sister beside me. The TV was on when I fell asleep. In my dream it was the same; the bed was there, the TV was on, and my sister was next to me, but something was wrong. I was afraid and screaming. I was trying to get up but I couldn't move. I was trying to pull out of the dream, which I finally did, but the dream made its appearance a second time. This time the door was slamming open and closed. I was afraid again and knew that something was at the bottom of the bed. I screamed and tried to wake up my sister but could not. I awakened, but fell back to sleep and dreamt the same thing yet again. The door was slamming open and closed with the wind, and something was pulling or tugging at the sheet from the bottom of the bed. The third time I succeeded in waking my sister up, and that ended the dream."

THE ANALYSIS

In this intriguing triptych dream the unknown beckons with an invisible hand. Even more frightening is that the dream is framed in reality. When dreams resemble conscious reality the dreamers are often mid-way between consciousness and sleep, and in a position to be able to direct their dreams. This is lucid or directive dreaming wherein dreamers still possess an element of control. Usually these dreams are seeking truth at its deepest level. Thus, the TV, as a watchful monitor of communication, signifies the wish to be mindful even while asleep. Whatever pulls and tugs at the dreamer's bedsheet draws attention to the dreamer beneath and symbolizes her quest for self-discovery. Something must be uncovered: the sheets pull back offering a view into what lies beneath the surface. As a bed is a womb symbol, the tugging and pulling of sheets may represent an ancient memory of the intrauterine birth experience.

In an exercise of self-mastery, not being able to move allows the dreamer to experience loss of control and the willful regaining of it.

No wonder that the dream ends when Marie-Chantal awakens within the dream, for the dream wish is to awaken in the most spiritual sense. The opening and closing of the door is symbolic of going back and forth from consciousness to unconsciousness. The door that never stops opening and closing also represents that nothing is final. In this optimistic view, what appears closed can be reopened again.

THE DREAM

"My dreams are always first class. And I'm always flying. In this dream I am flying on a plane (the Concorde, of course), with my friend, Mikhail Baryshnikov, to some exotic place—Bali and then on to Mt. Everest. I meet the most wonderful people on the plane and have great conversations above the clouds. We are jolly from the champagne, partying, and I wish that we never come down."

THE ANALYSIS

Social butterfly that she is, Nan's dream is airborne. Dreamt by anyone other than Nan this dream would be considered a wish. In Nan's case she is living her dream—living high, living fast, and definitely first class. Flying dreams generally represent an independent, free-thinking personality who strives to rise above mediocrity. As flying is against the law of gravity, the dreamer succeeds where others fail—Nan always maintains a sense of levity. Earthbound, mundane views are swapped for endless stretches of heavenly terrain that lead somewhere exotic.

Signifying the wish for clarity and honesty, conversations are above the clouds, and lucid—in a world where one means what one says. The champagne symbolizes Nan's vivacity and effervescence. The wish of never landing represents the ceaseless energy of a dreamer who will never become grounded.

NAN KEMPNER

PIERRE SALINGER

THE DREAM

*"In August 1982, I was on vacation in Corsica for one month when
I dreamt I heard in my brain the words 'You should be aware that one of
the worst terrorist attacks will take place in Paris in the last week.' I left
for Paris immediately, and the day after I arrived a bomb exploded in
a Jewish bakery."*

THE ANALYSIS

Having just been working for ABC covering terrorism, Mr. Salinger's dream is viewed as a measure of his conscientiousness, for his dream is deeply committed and connected to his work of the moment. Even on vacation, he cannot let down his guard. In no uncertain terms his dream commands him to be wary, to be vigilant of the evils of society. But, in that Mr. Salinger is half French, the dream may reflect some personal turmoil or upheaval, as the city of Paris is the dreamer himself. In other words, if a difficult situation is not dealt with—it will become explosive.

The prophetic nature of Pierre's dream cannot be discounted, as the dream's prediction actually occurred back in 1982 when a Jewish bakery was blown up in Paris. The dream must therefore be viewed as a measure of Mr. Salinger's intuitive nature. Yet, because of the biblical style in which the prophesy was worded, one wonders if the prophesy was referring to something that had not yet happened, since the phrase "in the last week" has biblical significance: a "week" would be interpreted as seven years, and the "last week" would allude to the end of days or Armageddon. Taking on a darker perspective, the "worst terrorist" would be a symbolic euphemism for the ultimate biblical demon, Satan.

Mr. Salinger first told me this dream in the afternoon of August 30, 1997, approximately six hours before an unspeakable tragedy occurred "in Paris, in August, in the last week"—the fatal car crash of Diana, Princess of Wales, and her companion, Dodi Fayed. Indeed, had not the frenzied pack of paparazzi, in hot pursuit, "terrorized" the car that desperately tried to speed away? More uncanny, is that at 4:00 P.M. E.S.T. I had serendipitously faxed Dodi's aunt, Soheir Khashoggi, Pierre's dream as a sample of my dream analyses. An eerie coincidence or a fateful prescient communication?

BROOKE ASTOR

THE DREAM

"Coming back from China when I was eleven, I felt different from other children—more British than American because those were the people I saw in China. Mother was busy, having just returned from Peking—father was busy with his job. Feeling rather alone, trying to adjust to my new life in Washington, it was Granny to whom I turned. She listened to all my complaints and gave me a feeling of security making me feel as though I was 'somebody.' Marrying young and moving to New York I saw very little of Granny who moved to her country home in Maryland. Busy running a household—trying to fit into what turned out to be an unfortunate marriage, I survived, though I forgot about Granny. But way back in my mind something was haunting me… Then one night I dreamt that I was walking down the street and I saw a very old lady walking with two sticks. She could hardly move and as I went up to help her, I noticed she looked just like Granny whom I loved very much (and who was now deceased). When I saw that it was Granny, I said 'Granny, I did not recognize you. Why are you looking this way? You are so thin now and I remember you being so active.' She glanced up at me and said nothing. 'Please forgive me,' I said. Finally she turned toward me and said, 'I look like this because the dead live through the thoughts of the living, and neither you, nor anyone else, have been thinking of me.'"

THE ANALYSIS

In this dream of responsibility, a painful realization comes forward on two sticks, and stick it does: young Brooke takes a cool, long look at her behavior, and chastises herself for thoughtlessness. When the dreamer meets up with her unrecognizable, deceased grandmother, self-interest brought on by an unfortunate marriage is exchanged for pathos and empathy. Wistfully, the grandmother that made Brooke feel like she was somebody now appears as a cane-wielding nobody.

The dreamer's question, "Why are you looking this way?" symbolizes Brooke's guileless disbelief over not having thought about her beloved granny, yet reveals a refreshing emotional honesty, Brooke's ability to be self-critical. Not being remembered has weakened the granny—she has two walking sticks because she needs someone to lean on, and something to hold onto. What is wonderful about Mrs. Astor's dream is the inversion of the idea behind it—the poetic notion that loving thoughts can make the recipient of those thoughts stand strong, and alter their state of being.

PARIS HILTON

THE DREAM

"When I was too young to drive I had this recurring dream where my sister and I took my parents' car in San Francisco. I was driving and we were going up and down all these huge hills, and all these little puppies were in the backseat, and I was afraid that we would crash or hurt someone because I couldn't stop the car, and I was also afraid that the police would come after us because I had no license."

THE ANALYSIS

Putting herself in the driver's seat of a car symbolizes the spunky underage dreamer's wish to take charge of her life, and to establish her own direction. There is the wish to go places without restrictions and to expose oneself to the dangers and risks, the ups and downs, the hilly terrain of growing up in the fast lane. Yet this wish is coupled with the need for containment. The wish to remain small and dependent is expressed through the little puppies who take a backseat to the ebullient personality seated up front. Brought along for the ride, the puppies represent Paris's wish to retain a part of her childhood sensibility. Thus, the dream is an ensemble of past and present: Paris and her puppies on opposite sides, but in the same car.

Not being able to stop the car reveals the dreamer's ceaseless drive but also her anxiety over where it will lead her. To the extent that Paris cannot brake, she is unbreakable or resilient. Yet, by fearing a crash, Paris is self-confrontational; there is a recognition of the need to sometimes be stopped in one's tracks to stay out of harm's way.

DAVID TANG

THE DREAM

"I often dream that I'm on a thin ledge of a high building, facing the building, looking down over my shoulder, hanging on by my hands, my fingers, having the feeling that I'm going to fall. I fall but then I wake up relieved."

THE ANALYSIS

The debonair Tang, much like Cary Grant in Hitchcock's *North by Northwest*, finds himself in a bone-chilling moment hanging on by his hands to a thin ledge of a high building. This is a dream of high anxiety. But whereas being on a ledge suggests one is courting disaster by taking chances in life, facing the building in such intimate proximity reveals the desire to identify with strength and structure. Hanging on signifies Tang's determination; hanging by one's fingers symbolizes stretching beyond one's limit, and represents the wish for expansion, extension and growth.

The dream expresses humility by reflecting upon mortality—allowing oneself to visualize mentally one's worst fear in order to overcome it. The fall represents the exhilarating wish to let go, to release one's grip and take that leap of faith. Awakening before the crash means Tang knows he will never hit bottom, and reveals an internal conviction that he will avert disaster. Looking over one's shoulder reflects the ancient wisdom of assessing what has happened in the past.

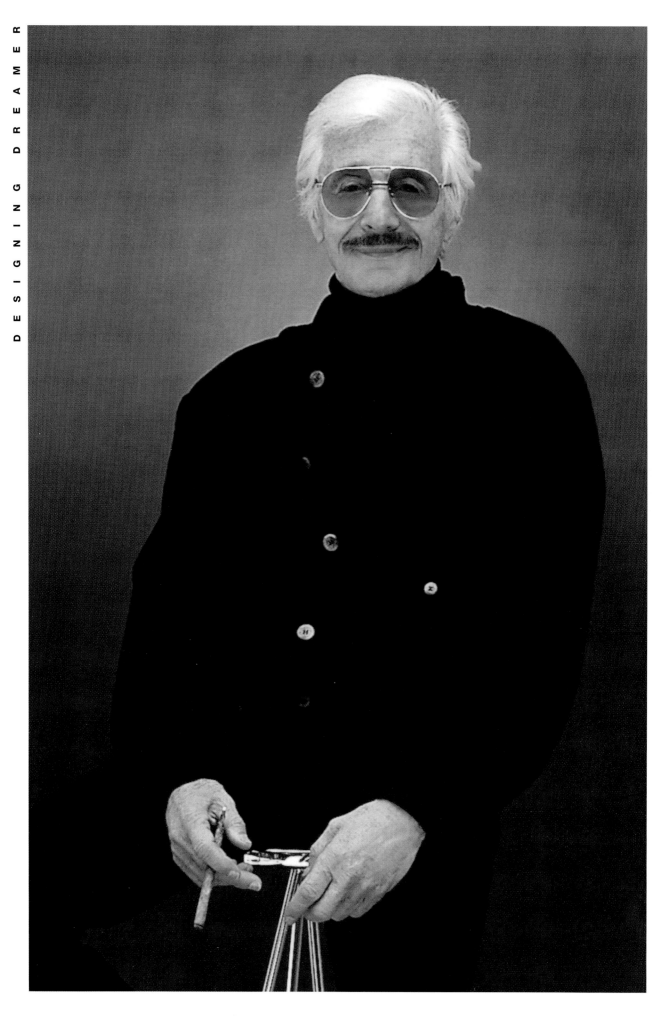

OLEG CASSINI

THE DREAM

"I have arrived by boat. Many people greet me with 'I'm so glad you could come.'
I'm in Hollywood surrounded by movie stars, recognizing faces from American
movies, like Clark Gable. A beautiful dark-haired actress with light eyes and golden
skin is in love with me. I'm a famous fashion designer."

THE ANALYSIS

Christmas, 1936, Cassini was living in fascist Italy, with war imminent, his way of life
disintegrating. But his dream was more than a wish—it was a prophesy, in that it all came true.
Cassini came to the United States, married the consummately beautiful movie star Gene
Tierney and became the fashion designer of choice, perhaps the most famous designer of the
century, whose name became a household word. The dream made Oleg aware of his own talents
and his desire to fulfill them. In other words, the dreamer's self knowledge inspired him with
the drive needed to fulfill his wish consciously. Surrounding himself by another world, another
setting, Oleg was able to recognize all that he wanted in life.

Arriving by boat reflects the wish to cross over to another world. The boat symbolizes
the rite of passage. Being welcomed from the water represents birth—a new life, a new start.
Importantly, Oleg's arrival has been noted: to have arrived means having become successful.
But the wish must be earned. By envisioning himself a fashion designer, Oleg will achieve his
dream, for a designer symbolizes someone with a scheme, plan, or purpose.

FREDERIC FEKKAI

THE DREAM

"I have a recurring dream where I am picturing acts of violence and destruction. Then I hear that an international committee has resolved all these wars, and the scene changes. People are out on the street smiling, looking happy. Skyscrapers on the street begin to soften and blur becoming more like Zen structures. Then I am in Paris on the boulevard St. Germain and I see big stores. One is Indian, the next Japanese, the next African, all alongside one another. Some of the shop windows look Asian, some look Western, some look European. People are colorful and wearing an imaginative new style of clothing influenced by what seems a cultural blending."

THE ANALYSIS

Master style-maker Frédéric Fekkai has dreamt a vision of the world where he has fashioned it into a far better place. Destruction is briefly disparagingly viewed to manifest and highlight its opposite… construction! To underscore that change is needed, Fekkai imaginatively symbolizes through architectural forms. The sharp edges of skyscrapers blur into Zen structures. In other words, strict and imposing tenets are merging into more accepting views. Wars have artfully been replaced by people who have embraced other ethnicities and cultures as their own, and everyone is part of a universal whole. Thus, the wish of the dream is for harmonious transformation.

Ways of living are coalescing, formalized structure is changing, having come under the influence of a more relaxed and peaceful lifestyle. The culturally diversified store-fronts symbolize the commonality of the soul of mankind, and, more important, the humane spirit of the dreamer. Fekkai's reverie presents him as flexible and open to suggestion, always looking to blend old concepts into something new. Fekkai's ultimate wish is for universal acceptance of his new and creative stylistic ideas.

THE DREAM

"Since my visit to China I have had a dream that keeps recurring. In the dream I am climbing the great wall of China and I keep climbing higher and higher than one is supposed to go, passing all the other people. Finally I am all alone standing there sensing the incredible history of the stones beneath my feet. I feel privileged to be there. Suddenly it starts to snow—silently—it is so beautiful and peaceful."

THE ANALYSIS

A recurring dream that repeats a real experience reveals the dramatic impact the experience had upon the dreamer's life. Lynn's upward climb symbolizes striving and the wish for ascension. Climbing beyond where one is supposed to go signifies the willful determination of the dreamer and a certain daring and curiosity. In a symbol of positivity, the future is limitless.

Standing alone reveals Lynn's independence, and signifies her innate individualism: she is at peace with herself and her place in the world. Yet once she has reached the summit, her thoughts become earthbound, attention is drawn to what is beneath her feet, as there is a deep spiritual sense of awe and humility. The snow is the wish for purification.

Whereas a wall usually symbolizes an impasse or restriction, Lynn's wall is used as a stepping-stone; what is perceived as difficult is dealt with and mastered, meaning that Lynn knows how to rise to the occasion.

LYNN WYATT

HUGH D. AUCHINCLOSS III

THE DREAM

*"I often dream of losing my date book, or of
looking for it and not being able to find it."*

THE ANALYSIS

Dreams of losing and mislaying an object are usually tied to intentional forgetting, wherein
the intention stems from a variety of reasons. As a date book records days and hours of
appointments, it symbolizes the passage of time—and specifically memory. Necessarily, certain
dates in the past are tied to circumstances that no longer want to be recalled, painful memories
we wish to be stricken from the record and certain future engagements that one would like
to avoid.

     Anxiety is awakened within dreamers because importance has been placed on the object
lost, such that losing a date book may reveal the sadness of no longer being able to contact those
one wishes to. Similarly, the lost date book symbolizes losing touch with good memories of the
past. Yet, losing the date book may also be viewed as a symbolic sacrifice wherein the dreamer
trades pages of his past in order to ward off some other dreaded loss. This signifies a defiant stand
against keeping one's final rendezvous with destiny, and suggests a willfulness to transcend time.
Looking for the date book symbolizes that Mr. Auchincloss contemplates what the future holds in
store for him. The dream also establishes his conscientious concern about fulfilling obligations.

DON KING

THE DREAM

"I was pondering the future when I heard a rumbling in my head. My hair was uncurling and going straight up, rising. Pim. Pim. Pim. Each hair shot up toward the heavens. I felt I was being pulled up by God."

THE ANALYSIS

Ever since the myth of Samson, hair has symbolized power. The power within Don's dream is connected to a transitional period in his life—it promotes liberation from a restricted state of being. The rumbling sound in his head, much like a Dionysian thunder rite, is celebratory. Whereas uncurling hair symbolizes the wish for release from constraints, and reflects an ideological change in progress, hair that extends represents the full growth potential of the individual. The individual hair strands shooting up toward the heavens represent the symbolic wiring in of the dreamer to the universe and his connection to a higher level. This is the wish to rise up in the world.

Although hair standing on end usually represents fear, the dream, in bold reversal of stereotypic imagery, transforms fear into feelings of grandiosity and empowerment. In other words, the dream undermines stereotypic thinking by not conforming to standard views. Moreover, as hair drawn upwards is against the law of gravity, this image reinforces Mr. King's individualism. Being pulled up by God is the wish for recognition. Mr. King claims that his hair looks the way it does today because his dream produced a change in his physical appearance. What is more significant is that his hair, combed upward, symbolizes the optimistic spirit he felt in his dream and feels in his life.

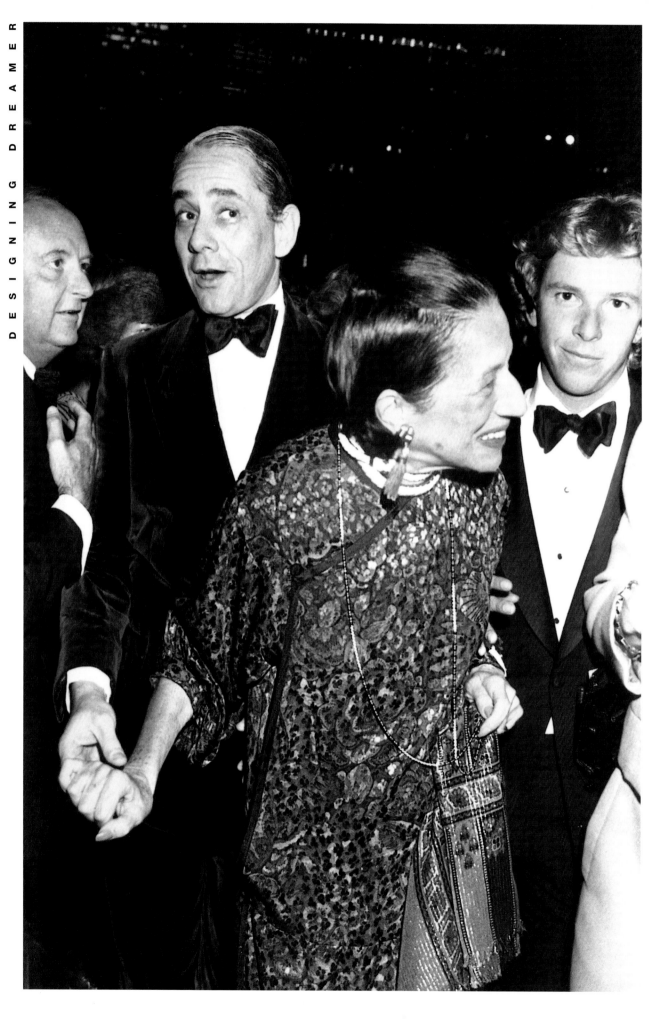

KENNETH J. LANE

THE DREAM

"In the prairie somewhere I see a freight train running along a track, but instead of holding coal in its car it has all the jewelry I have ever made, but without the stones. I watch as the freight car tilts back and the jewelry spills everywhere. Then I see a dumpster truck coming from the opposite direction, and it is carrying all of the stones. It stops next to the pile of jewelry, tilts back and spills the stones in a separate pile on the ground. I start the arduous task of putting back all the stones in their correct settings."

THE ANALYSIS

The freight train running along the track represents the passage of time moving forward at an alarming speed. The train stops in a form of symbolic death. But, in wish fulfillment, the prairie that represents the lonely emptiness of the great beyond becomes filled with the dreamer's life's work—the jewelry of his creation. The anxiety over leaving this world is heightened by the separation anxiety symbolized by the jewels' removal from their original settings. The prongs have not held something in place. But, as we shall see, in the lengthy process of refashioning his jewelry, the stones become the dreamer's tools with which to reassemble life and establish immortality.

On another level of interpretation, the loose stones represent the headstones of those that have already died. There is the wish to reconnect each shining essence (the individual soul) with the physical body of the jewelry, where reconnecting the stone with the jewelry serves as a symbolic form of resurrection.

BOAZ MAZOR

THE DREAM

"I dreamt I was fighting with a very old airline stewardess on TWA. I was hand-cuffed and led to a prison that looked like a huge aviary. I was very lonely there until I realized that my parrot Alfie was also there. I could see friends coming to visit with their own dogs, and parrots, and the place was full of very glamorous people sitting on rattan chairs like a club. Someone gave me a key to open the door to run away with them, fast, but I couldn't find Alfie. I kept saying, 'I can't run without my parrot' and everyone was screaming at me 'Come on. Run. RUN quick,' and I woke up.

THE ANALYSIS

As opposed to the plane having taken off, it is the dreamer who is taken off... in symbolic flight. Yet, although handcuffed and incarcerated, there is no way to ground or imprison Boaz, for the prison he is led to is an aviary, filled with feathered birds of flight. This visible plumage, this lightness of being, is what permits the dreamer to view his jail as a glamorous club.

In that birds of a feather flock together, the key that Boaz possesses is not used. Not being able "to run" without Alfie signifies not being able to function. The dreamer has already unlocked a realization: Alfie is a kindred spirit—the bird within the dreamer—a symbolic presence that can never be left behind. In other words, because there is a parroting, a mimicking of ways, there is no urgency to flee. For by remaining alongside his parrot muse, Boaz taps into something more important—the winged world of the imagination.

CHRISTOPHE LAMBERT

THE DREAM

"My favorite dream is one that recurs from time to time. I am underwater and everything is very clear and crisp. Very blue and very green like Technicolor should be. I am moving very fast through this antique city. Almost like I am swimming at the speed of a torpedo. There are fish. I do not know if I am a fish or if it is me. It is a great feeling."

THE ANALYSIS

Dashing Highlander Christophe Lambert travels within the lowlands beneath the sea, empowered and immortal as ever, loving the sensation of boundlessness and freedom. Submerged underwater, the dreamer delves within his psyche and reveals his thirst for self-knowledge. This symbolizes an introspective nature and the wish for clarity. Where there is no gravity there is no resistance to all that has been repressed. Being immersed in water reveals the depth of the dreamer who seeks what is underneath the surface superficialities of living. There is nostalgia for all that has been left behind. The ancient city, the quiet city of solitude within himself, is an excavation of his past.

    Underwater dreams are often birth fantasies wherein the dreamer has remembered some pleasurable intrauterine experience or atmosphere. These dreams reflect the wish for change or transformation from what is rigid and fixed to that which is fluid and alterable. Most important, with his feet off the ground Christophe is elevated in his element, unrestrained, and free from anything that can weigh him down. He is like a torpedo: on target, but self-directed.

DENIS LEARY

THE DREAM

"It's me and Madonna in the back seat of a NYC taxi. She turns to me and says, 'Will you breast-feed my baby?' Before I can say no, the driver shouts out 'I will!' The driver turns to face us—it's Al Roker. Suddenly the cab screeches to a halt and I find myself standing on the corner of First Avenue and Ninth Street, my old neighborhood. A bus pulls up and the doors swoosh open. The driver says 'Goin' Uptown?' I look up. The driver is Jenny McCarthy."

THE ANALYSIS

In Leary's dream, taxi and bus symbolism reflect transportation, movement, and direction—particularly moving from downtown to uptown—and suggest how far Dennis has come from his old neighborhood on Ninth Street (see photograph). The dream takes place within the taxi to symbolize the distance of the journey and the contentment on the part of the dreamer to be within the confines of a celebrity world—the taxi is peopled with Madonna and Al Roker. Weatherman, Mr. Roker, represents the weather itself—a powerful source of nature—as he is the driving force that takes Dennis back home. But the weather blows hot or cold—it can be your best friend or worst enemy—signifying life's uncertainties. Driving downtown is a regressive act the dreamer dispels by making the cab screech to a halt. The bus that pulls up provides Dennis a ride back uptown to the glamorous world of celebrities. For Jenny McCarthy is the bus driver, who, invitingly and sexually "swooshes open" her doors.

In a strange sexually charged request, Madonna asks Dennis to breast-feed her baby! By using reversal, Dennis wants Madonna to breast-feed him; by using displacement, Madonna is the baby that Dennis wants to breast-feed. This implies that Mr. Leary has in mind some other method of satisfaction. He has the concealed wish to substitute the breast for the male organ. Wow!

172

KAREEM ABDUL-JABBAR

THE DREAM

"I was home and I jumped into my body. I looked at my body directly and it was falling apart. I had an alarming feeling. I was looking inside my foot."

THE ANALYSIS

As an athlete's greatest fear is the non-functioning or disintegration of his body. This is a typical athlete's nightmare—for Kareem's body, as a symbol of his physical world, is falling apart. Long retired from the game, Kareem is able to see beyond his athletic career, and thus, beyond his body. His cerebral self wants to reintegrate with his physical self. But to get beyond his body, he must view it directly, from within. Thus, jumping inside his body depicts the mind/body split. In the past, Kareem jumped to make his patented sky hook while seeking to score; now he makes that leap of faith inside himself, seeking harmony and wholeness. Kareem dreams of self-discovery much in the same manner as someone who takes something apart to learn how to put it back together again.

Jumping into his body, Kareem symbolizes the basketball cliché of staying within himself. He shoots for self-critical evaluation or assessment. The dream impressively reveals Kareem's introspective need to understand the physical nature of things, to gain realizations, no matter how alarming they seem.

ALLEN GINSBERG

THE DREAM

"There was a bulge in my right side, this dream recently—just now I realize I had a baby, full grown that came out of my right abdomen while I in hospital with danger-ous hepatitis C. I lay there awhile, wondering what to do, half grateful, half appre-hensive. It'll need milk, it'll need exercise, taken out into fresh air with baby car-riage. Peter there sympathetic, he'll help me, bent over my bed, kissed me, happy a child to care for. What compassion he has. Reassured I felt the miracle was in Peter's reliable hands—but gee what if he began drinking again? No this'll keep him straight. How care for a baby, what can I do?"

THE ANALYSIS

Allen Ginsberg's last dream was dreamt the day before he was diagnosed with terminal cancer, one week before he died. The bulge in his stomach was a result of the cancer. The dream reflects Allen's altruistic thoughts regarding the well-being of his life partner, Peter Orlofsky.

Anxiety over being hospitalized with Hepatitis C has made Allen dream of surviving. Thus, the wish of the dream turns a dangerous, life threatening situation into a happy event. A fear of death is supplanted by a miraculous pregnancy—the bulge on Allen's right side is reassuringly self-diagnosed as a full-grown baby. In this view, the dreamer is only "half apprehensive"—the apprehension countered by feelings of gratefulness.

There is the intuitive sense that death is imminent, as the dream attempts to tie loose ends, and look for solutions. By giving Peter a child to look after, the poet imaginatively fills the projected void his absence will leave in the life of his significant other. Worry over Peter's drinking is squelched, as he believes that this child will keep Peter straight. The dream reveals Allen's considerate spirit, his humanity, his *raison d'être*.

Dreams of pregnancy are often associated with the creative process: the symbolic baby represents Allen's poetry, his body of work, his creation—all that will live in posterity.

LAUREN LAWRENCE

THE DREAM

"In 1989 I dreamt I was watching a fly approaching an inkwell filled with black ink. It hopped in as if taking a bath in the black liquid. When it emerged soaking wet, blackened, it moved toward a blank piece of paper lying on my desk, and I had the distinct impression that this fly was about to write something of great importance to me. But just as it began writing the telephone rang and awakened me."

THE ANALYSIS

As a fly is generally viewed as something small and insignificant, the wish of the dream is to add significance where there is none—and lend substance and depth to something trivial and lightweight. Having dreamt this in 1989 makes enormous sense to me for this was a time in my life when I was flitting about, driven around town in my Rolls Royce—a time when I was doing substantive damage to my husband's American Express card, when shopping and lunching were followed by shopping and dining.

In other words, something was bugging me—there certainly was a fly in the ointment that prevented me from feeling fulfilled. The proverbial ointment was ink because something had to be inked out—stated in bold black print. Thus the dream wish was to become introspective, analytic, questioning. I see now that I was that fly, diminished within the black interior world of my Silver Spur.

"Dreams are to the mind what weight lifting is to the body."

LAUREN LAWRENCE

"A dream is a blueprint of all the possibilities for our future."

DIANDRA DOUGLAS

"A dream is a gift from Freud."

ROGER STRAUSS

"Dreams are sacred… like the tap tap tap of an angel."

LYNN WYATT

"A dream you dream alone is only a dream, a dream we dream together is reality."

YOKO ONO

"A dream is a short journey into the unconscious."

DIANE VON FURSTENBERG

"A dream brings you one step closer to having to pay for analysis."

GRAHAM LAWRENCE

"A dream is the etiquette of the unconscious."

CHARLOTTE FORD

"A dream is food—food for thought."

SIRIO MACCIONI

"Dreams fuel the imagination and feed the mind."

CALVIN KLEIN

"A dream is a motivator."

MARIA BARTIROMO

"A dream is a cleanser of the brain."

MARIO BUATTA

"A dream has the logic of a movie."

JULIAN SCHNABEL

"Dreams are like love affairs. Most are inconsequential, but a few are full of meaning."

ANTHONY HADEN GUEST

"A dream unleashes our most daring imagination in an interlude where hope collides with passion."

MUFFIE POTTER ASTON

"A dream is something that drives you crazy ten minutes after you wake up because you remember it was kind of wild and special and not quite like you in 'real' life but right after you open your eyes, the plot disappears... you can't save the texture of a dream."

HELEN GURLEY BROWN

"A dream is a reflection of our past and our emotional reaction to it."

THE HONORABLE ROBERT MOSBACHER

"A dream is a gossamer thread connecting this life with the heavenly part of eternal life, and most certainly not with its alternative."

LETITIA BALDRIDGE

"Dreams make thoughts come alive."

SENATOR CLAIBORNE PELL

DECLINATIONS

Upon my request for a dream, those that declined said...

Fran Lebowitz:	"I don't sleep."
Donald Trump:	"I don't have time to sleep let alone dream, I'm too busy building back my empire."
Henry Kissinger:	"It's not my style."
Hon. Francis Kellogg:	"I am not a believer in the occult."
Walter Matthew's agent:	"Walter Matthew doesn't dream."
Author:	"Surely he must have dreamt when he was a child."
Walter Matthew's agent:	"Walter Matthew was never a child."
Maria Riva, daughter of Marlene Dietrich:	"Marlene Dietrich never dreamt in her younger days. Later, alcohol-induced dreams never stayed the distance to sobriety. She would often invent dreams, to please those who needed to hear them. Had my mother dreamt, it would most likely have been of knackwurst and sauerkraut, with thick black bread and cold, sweet butter."
Glenn Close:	"If I gave you my dream it wouldn't be my dream anymore."
Scottie Pippen:	"I do not dream, because I am living my dream."
Sergei Kruschev:	"My father would never dream. And we would never speak of dreams. I, myself, do not remember having any, except small fragments that were always silly and meaningless."
Philip Johnson:	"My buildings are my dreams."
Michael Nouri:	"My dreams are always sexual, too much to speak about."
Tommy Lee Jones:	"My dreams are not fit to read."
Dominick Dunne:	"I applaud your book. I know it will be fascinating. But I simply do not relate to dreams."
Woody Allen:	"This is not the kind of thing I do, but it's fun reading someone else's dreams."

ACKNOWLEDGMENTS

I am immensely grateful to Martine and Prosper Assouline for fulfilling my dream, to Mathilde Dupuy d'Angeac for turning that dream into an exquisitely designed book, to Harry Benson for his unparalleled generosity and for his wonderful photographs taken on some of the hottest days of the summer. Heartfelt appreciation to Patrick McMullan and Ellen Graham for their entrancing images, and for traipsing around town with me. I thank *The New York Daily News* for their kind permission to reprint the following dreams that ran in my "Dreams" column: Michael Douglas, Jackie Mason, Denis Leary, Anthony Quinn. Many thanks to all those who trusted me with their dream intimacies, especially to Peter Beard for his immense enthusiasm. Profuse thanks to Mrs. Vincent Astor, Nan Kempner, Carolyne Roehm, Paris Hilton and Princess Marie Chantal of Greece who not only opened the doors of their psyches but graciously opened the doors of their bedrooms. And special thanks to Kathy Hilton for artfully rearranging the demanding schedules of her daughter. There are no words that can properly reveal my immense gratitude to Larry King, a true angel. An immeasurable debt of gratitude to my inspirational editor, Dorothée Walliser.

Lauren Lawrence
New York City,
October 2001

DREAM ARCHANGELS

Prosper and Martine Assouline, Dorothée Walliser, Ausbert de Arce, and everyone who contributed a dream, especially Harry and Gigi Benson, Peter Beard, and my hero, Larry King.

DREAM ANGELS

Patrick Demarchelier, François Hallard, Brigitte Lacombe, Mario Testino, Anders Overgard, Ellen Von Unwerth, Oberto Gili, Gavin Bond, Mert Alas & Marcus Piggot, Greg Gorman, Sante D'Orazio, Angelo Frontoni, Robert Frank, Patrick McMullan, Leslie Hassler, Ellen Graham, Leilani Ferrer, Thierry Bouet, Mark Arbeit, Jeff Katz, Frank Yarbrough, Allen Malschick, Manuelle Toussaint, Frank Veronsky, Yoko Ono, Hugh D. Auchincloss III, Leslie Allan-Rice, Patrick McMullan, Anita Antonini, Ellen Graham, Alison Jackson, Karen Carpenter, Jean Jack L'Heriter, Laure du Pavillon, Berange Broman, Diane Prete, Kara Vanderweg, Bridie Picot, Kara Sutherland, Cyndi Goldman, Valerie Martinez, Suzette Kealen, Wendell Marvyama, Luisella Meloni, Carol Leflufy, Poull O'Brien, Rob Wilson, Lynn Russo Cohn, Michael Flutie, Len Evans, Liz Rosenberg, Beth Mann, Pat Hackett, Muffy Potter Aston, Xochitl Olivas, John F. Kennedy Jr., Najma Beard, Jacqueline Schnabel, Sid Bernstein, Larry Geller, Martha Kramer, John H. Davis, Gale Hayman, Liba Icahn, Kathy Hilton, Liz McNeil, Tasos, Nick Jarecki, David Patrick Columbia, Nancy Ryder, Blake Brooks, Cari Ross, Gerry Harrington, Celine de la Pena, David Unger, Aalayah Madyun, John Dellaverson, Mathew Gifford, Jill Fritzo, Stan Rosenfeld, Jason Sharpe, Antonia Short, John Gnerre, Patrick Flynn, Tia Ernst, Louise Spinner, Johnny Planco, Suzanne Goodson, Casey Aden-Wansbury, Ivan Ontiveros, Jacqueline Coumans, Ari Zakarian, Gene Sunik, Pat Mork, Debby Zealley, David Lawrence, Roger Webster, Curt Fritzeen, Tom Moffett, Jolee Hirsch, Charles Michael Smith, Carol Lupo, Alejandra Soler-Ruig Juncadella, Laurie Smith, Arlene Dahl, Helen Gurley Brown, Letitia Baldrige, Dr. Gerald Freiman, Mark Colman, Antonia Giannaris, Dr. Theodore Giannaris, Donna Coulling, Sharon Schieffer, Heather Cohane, James B. Hill, Allan Goodrich and Ludovic Autet.

PHOTO CREDITS